# THE *Inspired* Wedding

# THE *Inspired* Wedding

## SEVEN HANDCRAFTED THEMES FOR YOUR BIG DAY

Emma Arendoski

SELLERS
PUBLISHING

Portland, Maine

*dedication*

To my husband Andrew
and our son, Andrew Francis,
my entire world.

Published by Sellers Publishing, Inc.
Layout & Design copyright © 2014 Sellers Publishing, Inc.
Text copyright © 2014 Emma Arendoski
All rights reserved.

Sellers Publishing, Inc.
161 John Roberts Road,
South Portland, Maine 04106
Visit our Web site: www.sellerspublishing.com
E-mail: rsp@rsvp.com

Edited by Robin Haywood
Production by Charlotte Cromwell
Cover design by Rita Sowins, Sowins Designs

ISBN-13: 978-1-4162-0889-1
Library of Congress Control Number: 2012945288

Credits:
*Front cover:* © 2014 Justin Battenfield
www.justinbattenfield.com
*Back cover:* Clockwise from top right, © 2014 Michelle
Gardella Photography; © 2014 Carolyn Scott Photography
www.carolynscottphotography.com; © 2014 Michelle
Gardella Photography; © 2014 Justin Battenfield; © 2014
Shillanwna Ruffner Photography www.shillawnaruffner.com;
© 2014 Carolyn Scott Photography; © 2014 Carolyn Scott
Photography.

(Credits continued on page 282)

10 9 8 7 6 5 4 3 2 1

Printed and bound in China.

# CONTENTS

*Seven Handcrafted Themes for Your Big Day*

Introduction...9    Good Things to Know...11

### ROMANTICALLY VINTAGE...15

Wedding trends come and go, but a vintage-themed wedding celebrates classic elements and enduring details that bring forth the best of today and of decades past.

### 55...FARMHOUSE RUSTIC

A rustic wedding is homespun goodness at its finest. Immerse yourself in more than 150 ideas for a wedding celebration on a farm, in a field, or in the woods.

### BEACH BLISS...101

Sand, sunshine, and gently rolling waves . . . what's not to love about the beach? It's no surprise that a beach-themed wedding has become a popular choice for couples.

## URBAN CHIC...139

Do you love city life? Do you dream of getting married in a loft? On a rooftop? Or inside an art gallery or museum? Do you thrive on creative impulse? An urban wedding may be just the theme for you.

## 177...FREE SPIRIT

You're not the type to fuss over frills or swoon over soft palettes; you're looking for something different. If you're going against the herd and you don't want to play by the rules, you've come to the right place.

## TRADITIONAL...217

You love time-honored customs and rituals, and you want to adhere to conventional wedding practices, just not all the time. I'll show you how to mix personal touches with fresh variations and one-of-a-kind details.

## 253...BOHO STYLE

This style is expressed in a relaxed aesthetic. It's pleasantly reminiscent of a bygone era of head scarves, gauzy dresses, and loose hairstyles. It's a touch of floral and a pinch of ethnic, with a romantic hippie influence. Creativity and nature are celebrated in all aspects of boho style.

Afterwords...281     Credits...282

Index...284     Acknowledgments...288

# Introduction

My name is Emma Arendoski, and I am the founder and editor in chief of Emmaline Bride (www.emmalinebride.com), a blog dedicated to all things handmade for your wedding.

Why handmade? A handmade piece is special — it's been crafted with love and care, which can't be said for most mass-produced items. When planning my own wedding, I wanted every element to reflect our personalities — but store-bought finds fell short of my expectations. Online, however, I discovered an abundance of beautiful, handmade goods, along with unlimited opportunities for customization. I was so inspired that I decided to create a place where other brides could experience the special qualities that handmade items bring to a wedding. Emmaline Bride became that place.

I'm a romantic at heart; I love weddings, and I love being married. I am also proud to be involved in a business that can have a positive impact, and that can be a source of encouragement about what really matters on your wedding day.

I think it's safe to assume that if you are reading this, you are most likely engaged. Congratulations! Chances are, your wedding plans are just beginning. If your interest was sparked when you saw this book, then you are probably looking for creative ideas and inspiration for your big day.

At Emmaline Bride, I share the best in handcrafted wedding items from artisans around the world. Every day, I blog about wedding trends, do-it-yourself projects, and modern twists on traditional wedding customs. I include photographs from real weddings, featuring couples whose wedding celebrations reflect their unique personalities, from start to finish.

I have the honor of working with the best wedding professionals in the business, including artisans who create one-of-a-kind pieces, wedding photographers who record the moment the bride and groom look into each other's eyes and say "I do," and planners who turn wedding dreams into reality. I eat, sleep, and blog about weddings, and my career has become one of the most fulfilling aspects of my life. Of course, without my amazing readers, Emmaline Bride wouldn't be where it is today. I count on you — so thank you, from the bottom of my heart. And if you're new to Emmaline Bride, please drop by and say hello. I would love to hear from you — and to help you plan the best day of your life.

*The Inspired Wedding* has been a joy to work on. It's a compilation of seven wedding themes that I have carefully chosen to be in this book. A theme is not just eye candy — it's the main course for your wedding. In the following pages, you'll find fresh ideas for your ceremony and reception, along with everything in between, including what to wear, what type of invitations to send, and what wedding favors to give to your guests. You'll be inspired by the gorgeous photography, featuring unique venues, customized decor, and handmade items for every theme. You'll also find tips on how to take your own wedding ideas from imagination to fruition. And to help you as you plan, I've included a Resources page at the end of each chapter, where you can find the names and Web sites of the designers and vendors that were mentioned.

I've poured my heart into this book, and I hope you'll love reading it as much as I've enjoyed putting it together.

xo E.

# Good Things
## to know

As you begin the wedding-planning process, you will need to make a few general decisions. Here are some guidelines and definitions to help you get started.

## choosing a color palette & decorative motifs

Your personal preferences, the style of your wedding, and the nature of your venue can guide your color choices. (For example, think about how your desired color palette might look with the existing carpet, wallpaper, and draperies in the ceremony or reception space.)

In general, three colors are chosen: one dominant color; a second, supporting color; and a third, accenting color. You could select complimentary colors (opposites on the color wheel, like yellow and purple), analogous colors (neighbors on the color wheel, like blue and green), or monochromatic colors (different intensities of the same shade).

The bold, accenting color can be used throughout your wedding, from the invitations to the reception. For instance, choose the same bright hue for your envelope lining, ring-bearer pillow, flower-girl hair ribbon, fabric bouquet handles, bow ties, reception signage, and centerpiece flowers.

Similarly, motifs can be used to reinforce your wedding theme. Use these decorative symbols in your invitation suite, signage, centerpieces, and reception decor. Some themes bring motifs to mind immediately, such as shells, sailboats, or starfish for a beach-themed wedding. If your theme does not lend itself to such clear-cut motifs, use personalization (like your monogram or photos from your courtship) or a favorite pattern (like quirky polka dots) instead.

## the invitations

Regardless of your wedding theme, you will need to order (or to make) certain stationery items:

- Save-the-date card: A save-the-date card includes the date and general location of the wedding; the invitation will follow. For an out-of-town or "destination" wedding, mail your save the dates about six months before the event. For a local wedding, mail them three to four months in advance.

Mail your invitations six to eight weeks before your wedding. It includes:

- Outer envelope: The outer envelope can be hand addressed to the recipient, stamped, and hand cancelled at the post office.
- Invitation and inner envelope: Write the guest's name on the inner envelope, and enclose the invitation.
- Reply card and matching envelope, or reply postcard: The reply card allows each guest to indicate whether he or she will be in attendance. The reply-card envelope is stamped and addressed to you. Or, a stamped, addressed reply postcard may be used instead.
- Map (optional): If your wedding is in a faraway place, or in an urban area that might be difficult for some guests to navigate, include a map with directions to the ceremony and the reception.

### OTHER STATIONERY ITEMS

- Escort cards: At the reception, escort cards show each guest his or her table assignment. You can display an individual card for each guest; a card for each table, with a list of the guests' names; or a handwritten sign (such as a chalkboard) with the seating information.
- Table numbers: At the reception, a table number identifies each table, so that guests can find their assigned seating. For a fun alternative, use words (such as the titles of beloved books, songs, or movies) instead of numbers.
- Place cards: At the reception, a place card with the guest's name is positioned at the guest's table setting.

- Thank-you cards: After the wedding, you will be sending a thank-you card to each guest. The thank-you cards should coordinate with your invitation suite.
- Ceremony program: A ceremony program is not absolutely necessary, but it can be a nice addition to, and a keepsake of, your wedding day. Traditionally, the front cover features your names, the officiant's name, the wedding date, and the location. Inside, you can introduce both families and your wedding party, and list the musical selections and any readings.

# Romantically Vintage

If enduring details and vintage decor tug at your heartstrings, a "romantically vintage" wedding theme may be the perfect choice for you. Wedding trends come and go, but a vintage-themed wedding celebrates classic, timeless elements and attire that never go out of style. As an adjective, "vintage" refers to the best of its kind, which is why vintage cars, movies, and wines are able to maintain and even increase their value over time. In this chapter, I'll show you how to create a handcrafted, vintage-style wedding that brings forth the best qualities of today and of decades past.

# Invitations & More

As you begin to choose the elements for your theme, I recommend that you determine the perfect color palette first. Why? Because many decisions will be made on the road to your beautiful wedding, and having your color palette in place will make the process much easier. You can showcase the colors in your palette in several different areas, such as the design of your invitation (and other paper goods), floral arrangements, and accessories. Let's begin with the invitations.

## save the dates & invitations

While it's true that the primary purpose of the wedding invitation is to inform your guests and invite them to your upcoming nuptials, it can also be so much more. There is nothing more important in setting the tone of your wedding than a proper invitation. In today's modern, technologically advanced world, a vintage-themed wedding invitation that has been hand stamped and mailed is a gesture your guests will notice.

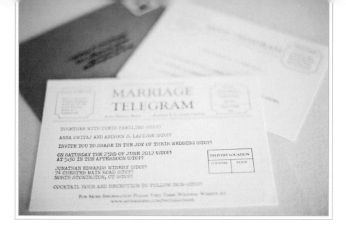

Before you start shopping for save the dates and matching invitations, you'll want to pick a central theme or style that reflects your favorite era or vintage aesthetic. Looking back at the previous century, you'll find that each decade has distinctive characteristics. For instance, if you're planning a 1920s Gatsby-inspired theme, you may want to consider Art Deco-inspired fonts, flapper-influenced graphics, geometric patterns, and coordinating enclosures of black, gold, or white.

While the telegram may be obsolete, it still carries an air of romance and charm. See how the designer from Pistachio Press incorporated that era into her work, above.

The 1950s were known for fun prints and eye-catching graphics. For a '50s-era invitation, you could use an emblematic motif such as a vinyl record, or a Polaroid-style photograph, like this design from Ello There, bottom left.

For couples who are looking for a modern-meets-vintage design, check out this suite of save-the-date cards, invitations and envelopes, response cards, and thank-you cards by Jen Simpson Design, bottom right. I adore everything about this ensemble — the kraft-paper envelopes; the bold fonts; the palette of pink, mint, and ivory; and the whimsical clip art. The pink-and-white straws are a fun and useful component that could be incorporated into your reception.

Swoops of cursive typography provide the ultimate romantic touch in this invitation set, also by Jen Simpson Design, opposite, and in the suite below from Amanda Day Rose.

When you're shopping for (or designing your own) invitations, try to use the same motif throughout your stationery and on some of your decor. Favorite vintage motifs include ribbons or antique lace, estate jewelry (such as cameos), teapots or teacups, chandeliers, a crochet-lace pattern, an "airmail" design, or an aged, "tea-stained" effect.

### ELEMENTS OF STYLE

Once you've picked out the perfect invitation and finalized your guest list, it's time to think about adding some personal touches to your stationery.

For a lovely effect, address the envelopes by hand. To evoke nostalgic charm, seal the back of each envelope with a wax stamp, and finish the look with a vintage postage stamp. You can order custom postage stamps with a vintage design, or even send your engagement photograph to a Web site like Zazzle, which can create U.S. Postal Service–approved postage stamps.

If you'd like to buy actual vintage stamps for invitations or as part of your decor, try Kenmore Stamp Company, Champion Stamp Company, or the ubiquitous eBay, where you can purchase postage stamps from collectors around the world.

# The Ceremony

What is your dream vintage-wedding location? A rose garden? Aboard a classic cabin cruiser? A Victorian mansion? Or perhaps it's one of my favorites: a vineyard (since vintage weddings and vintage wines go hand in hand)?

Vintage weddings have an ethereal quality, a sense of familiarity. When you think about a location, consider a favorite place from childhood or from your courtship. A historic building or garden, an inn, a museum, or even a backyard are all possibilities.

The venue does not have to be fancy; a church hall or a park with a tented reception can be a lovely location. With just the right decorations in place, you'll see how any space is transformed into a romantically vintage setting.

## decor

When designing your ceremony space, think about a focal point. The focal point is where you'll exchange your vows (and where many photos will be taken). For a cohesive event, make sure that this center of attention ties in with your vintage theme.

If your ceremony venue does not offer an appropriate backdrop or focal point, make your own! The most memorable vintage backdrops are those that incorporate unconventional accent pieces, like a wall of stacked suitcases or an antique chandelier, above left. Use vintage doors or weathered windows as a focal point, and string a lace garland across them as an accent piece.

A pipe-and-drape system can be used to hang a multitude of ribbons by knotting the ends to the top so the ribbons can hang. (Light-pink and white satin ribbons are always a winning combination for this theme.) Prefer fabric? Hang vintage white-lace tablecloths. This look can be done on a dime, since inexpensive lace tablecloths can be purchased at estate sales or thrift shops. Sheer white window panels are easy to find at any big-box store. You can leave the fabric as is or display vintage photographs across it. If you don't have vintage photos to use, a fun alternative would be to print black-and-white photographs of loved ones. You could even make black-and-white copies of your parents', future in-laws', and grandparents' wedding photographs. Or, you could incorporate vintage furniture into the backdrop, and place photos in antique frames atop an armoire, dresser, or side table.

One of the prettiest backdrops I've ever seen was a weathered fireplace mantel that had been painted white, with an array of candles placed inside the firebox. You could also arrange flowers in antique vases (using soft, romantic colors), and then position the vases on the mantel and on either side of the firebox.

Want more inspiration? Hang these unconventional accents to create a focal-point wall: antique china plates; skeleton keys tied to ribbon or twine; small, antique bud vases; vintage bunting; or garlands made from vintage fabric or handkerchiefs.

Once you've determined the perfect focal point, it's time to design the aisle.

How many guests will you seat at your ceremony? If there are benches or chairs already in place at your venue, that's perfect. If not, consider seating guests in nontraditional or even slightly mismatched antique chairs. (I've seen weddings that have pulled this look off beautifully, with the help of a furniture-rental company.) You could mix wooden folding cafe chairs padded with vintage fabric cushions or with upholstered dining chairs, either for the entire seating area or exclusively for a "reserved" section at your venue.

At the entrance of your ceremony, include a large tub of vintage handkerchiefs — each rolled and tied with a ribbon — for those tears of joy.

An antique rug or lengths of fabric or lace can be constructed into a beautiful aisle runner. Sprinkle colorful rose petals across it, either before the ceremony or during, courtesy of your flower girl.

Aisle markers or aisle decor can be simple and easy to create. Consider using shepherd's hooks to hang birdcages filled with garden roses or flower-filled tin buckets, right.

Repurposed antiques make perfect aisle decor for vintage-style weddings. Unexpected accents like ceramic milk jugs, stoneware pitchers, resin urns, vintage tea or coffee canisters, or white pedestal bowls can be filled with flower arrangements and placed along the aisle.

For your ceremony programs, be sure to use classic details from your featured era. If you'd like to DIY the programs, get started by choosing colors from your palette, a motif or two, and adornments such as satin ribbons, antique keys (to your heart!), or small pieces of costume jewelry. There are lots of program formats to choose from: a booklet; one-page, light-weight card stock that's been die cut into a fabulous shape; or even a fan (especially nice if your ceremony is during the summer). If you're short on time and not interested in taking on a big project, print a simple program from your computer onto vintage-inspired parchment paper, roll it into a scroll, and tie it with a ribbon or piece of lace.

## flower girl & ring bearer

The flower girl can carry a traditional woven basket or a wire basket filled with rose petals. Or, get creative with a lightweight teapot, a small birdcage, a vintage bucket, a tea or coffee tin, or a wooden trug.

Much like the flower girl, the ring bearer can carry a vintage-themed alternative. A simple, white ring pillow can be embellished with an antique charm, a brooch, a lace rosette secured with hot glue, antique buttons, or a heart cut out from a vintage handkerchief and hand sewn onto the top of the pillow. Or, the rings can be held in an antique ring box; tied to the handle of a teacup or the loop of a old-fashioned padlock, using ribbon or string; or hidden inside a decades-old, hollowed-out, hardcover book.

An embroidery hoop is one of my favorite items for carrying the rings up the aisle. You can create your own small embroidery hoop, customized with your names or the wedding date. Or, order a custom-designed hoop from Miniature Rhino. After the ceremony, the embroidery hoop can be displayed in your home as a remembrance of the day.

# wedding-party gifts

Before the ceremony, it is customary to give each member of your wedding party a gift as a token of your appreciation. For a vintage-themed wedding, there is nothing more appropriate than a gift from your chosen era, whether it's a true antique or a lovely reproduction.

### BRIDESMAIDS

When shopping for your bridesmaids' gift, look for inspiration from your theme. For example, a 1920s-style wedding might incorporate Art Deco jewelry as a gift, such as a pair of rhinestone earrings, a crystal hair comb, or a silver cocktail ring. For any era, a genuine antique — like a locket, a beaded coin purse, a bib "statement" necklace, a powder compact, or a pewter hand mirror — would make a perfect keepsake. Or, put her in a celebratory mood with a bottle of wine or Champagne with a custom label.

## GROOMSMEN

Some retro-themed groomsmen's gifts include: a vintage beer tankard, antique cuff links, an initialed money clip, a leather shaving bag, a vintage lighter (like a brass tube lighter or pocket lighter), a tie clip, an antique pocket watch, a tobacco pipe, vintage whiskey glassware, and a bottle of aged liquor.

## FLOWER GIRL & RING BEARER

When you're selecting a keepsake gift for your flower girl, consider something she can wear, like a vintage locket or a small brooch (which can be worn as a pin or a hair accessory). She'll love a vintage piece of jewelry she can hold on to — and maybe even reuse as "something old" on her wedding day. An accessory that makes her feel like a princess — a tiara, a strand of pearls, or a vintage hair comb — is a gift she can wear and keep for years to come.

Give the ring bearer an item he can use well into the future, like a tie clip or pair of vintage cuff links.

Since the flower girl and ring bearer may not see these vintage items as "gifts" (at least not at their current age), you could also offer them a wrapped toy or book that they will enjoy right now.

# The Attire

One of the most notable parts of a vintage wedding is its attire. From old-fashioned styles to twists on classic looks, you'll find it all in this section. First, let's begin with the bride.

## the bride

Vintage wedding dresses come in an array of styles, and as with all other components of your wedding, the time period you've chosen will guide your selection. Sometimes dresses of the era can be scooped up at resale shops, or you can add your own authentic twist to a brand-new dress by incorporating period lace or elegant beadwork, or by pairing your gown with a ruffled piece, like the one above left.

Look online for images of vintage wedding dresses. Make notes of what you're looking for, and then search the Web, browse on eBay, or shop for a reproduction online at Etsy, BHLDN, or Ruche.

Your best resource might be even closer at hand: ask your mom, aunt, or grandmother about her wedding gown, and if it's available (and suitable for your theme), try it on. You never know — it might just be the perfect dress.

If a family member is willing, perhaps you could borrow some vintage accessories for your ensemble. A pair of antique earrings, a strand of pearls, a vintage handkerchief or lace parasol, or the handbag your relative carried on her own wedding day are just a few of the items that would add charm to your event.

Vintage brooches can be attached to a dress sash or repurposed as shoe clips. A brooch can also be pinned onto your bag or bouquet handle. Use hot glue to add a comb backing to a brooch, and wear it as a hair accessory.

If you're considering a wedding garter, look for one with embellishments, like rosettes or antique lace. To make your own "heirloom" garter, use antique lace and add vintage earrings, pins, or antique lockets from resale shops (or from your own jewelry box). An elastic band for the garter's base can be found at any craft store.

When shopping for veils, look for period styles like a Juliet cap, a pillbox hat, a bandeau veil, a birdcage veil, or a jeweled bandeau. True antique or vintage veils are off-white or ivory in color; if your dress is pure white, use a reproduction instead.

With its antique lace trim, raw silk chiffon, feathers, ivory tulle, gold rhinestones, and silk chiffon ribbon, this ultra-girly pink bow (below right, from Emici Bridal) is a hair accessory that mixes vintage and modern elements beautifully.

## the groom

What will the groom wear to the wedding? First, consider your specific era, as there may be several attire options from which to choose. If you have a particular time period in mind, dress accordingly; but if your aim is solely "vintage," stick to old-fashioned favorites, like a black-tie ensemble, which includes a three-piece suit or tuxedo with black dress pants, a black suit coat, a vest, a white dress shirt, and a black bow tie. If the groom wants to differentiate himself from the groomsmen, he can wear a bow tie or vest in a color from your palette instead of black or wear a different style of boutonniere or pin on his jacket.

Depending on the selected time period, the choice of collar style can help achieve a particular look. Browse different options like a classic collar, a round collar (one with a rounded point), a turned-down collar (a folded collar which points down), a wingtip collar, or a standard point collar. Just as collar styles changed during different decades, so did cuffs and lapels. Lapel styles include notch, peak, and shawl; there are square, round, two- or three-button, notch, and angle-cut cuffs. Pair a set of vintage cuff links with your selected cuff. For footwear, high-polished oxfords are a classic choice.

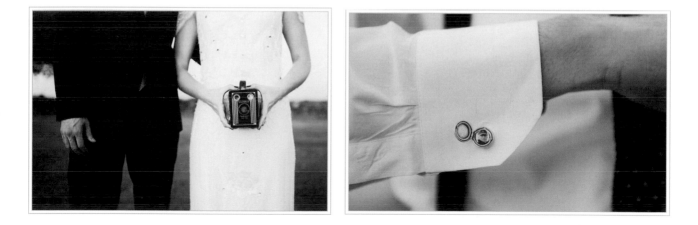

The accessories he selects are just as important as the attire. In the past, it was commonplace for men to wear hats everywhere they went. In the 1920s, men wore flat caps, a trilby, or a derby and by the 1960s, a Stetson fedora or a pork pie (similar to a fedora, but with a flat top) were popular. An antique pocket watch, a vintage tie bar or tie tack, or a pair of vintage suspenders are other suggestions. To find these items, look for estate-jewelry sales or in thrift stores, or borrow accessories from a family member (maybe a grandfather?). Or, look on eBay and Etsy in their "vintage" sections. Finally, add a pocket square; in many decades, it was the finishing touch to the ensemble.

## the wedding party

Once you've decided what you and your groom will wear, it's time to dress your leading ladies and gentlemen in attire that will fit your vintage theme.

### BRIDESMAIDS

If a 1950s look is what you have in mind, skip the typical, solid-color dress styles for bridesmaids, and opt for patterns and floral fabrics instead — or use the fabric for a sash, bouquet wrap, or small clutch bag. A shorter hemline is suitable for this retro-inspired theme.

Of course, floral prints and quirky patterns aren't your only choices; soft, romantic dresses with lots of lacy layers will evoke a classic 1920s style. Look for taupe, blush, or champagne-colored fabric, depending on your color palette.

If you prefer to have bridesmaid dresses custom made, you can purchase vintage cloth — sometimes available by the bolt — at resale shops or from online retailers. For handmade dresses that resemble garments of past decades, but that are made from modern fabrics, check out an online store like Fleet Collection. Another option is ModCloth, a large, online retailer with pretty, vintage-inspired clothing and accessories.

To complete their romantically vintage ensembles, gift your girls with a luxurious pashmina (weather permitting), or a faux-fur shawl or stole (for a winter wedding).

## GROOMSMEN

When outfitting your groomsmen in retro attire, browse thrift stores or resale shops for inspiration, or look online for vintage-style accessories, such as suspenders, bow ties, cuff links, vests, and linen driver's caps. You can also look online for accurate colors and styles of men's shirts from your selected era (maybe a pale pink?). Find authentic vintage vests, ties, and suit coats at thrift shops and estate sales.

If a total vintage look doesn't fit a groomsman's personality, a tailored suit is always in style.

## FLOWER GIRL & RING BEARER

For your smallest female attendant, look for a classic white dress that borrows an accent from your gown, such as the beadwork, buttons, sleeves, or lace details.

Other options include a flower-girl tutu, worn with a lace bodice that can be accented with lace sleeves and a matching headband, or a tiered ruffle dress.

The ring bearer can wear a suit or outfit that coordinates with the groomsmen, or wear a vintage-style look that's uniquely his own. For example, try a pair of dress pants, a button-down shirt, a bow tie, suspenders, a vest, and a newsboy hat. Or, choose a pair of linen pants, a button-down shirt, and a waistcoat.

Now that everyone's dressed for the part, let's move on to the flowers.

# The Flowers

Have you ever wondered why a bride carries a bouquet down the aisle? In some of the earliest weddings — when people bathed more infrequently — the bride carried an aromatic bouquet of flowers to ensure that she smelled nice. As centuries passed (and, thankfully, people began to bathe more often), carrying a bridal bouquet became a tradition. People also believed that the bride possessed good luck on her wedding day, and the bouquet became a vessel through which she would "transfer" good luck by tossing her bouquet to another lovely lady. It's fascinating to see how wedding traditions have changed (or endured) through the years, and how the bouquet has remained such a popular accessory for the bride.

## bouquets & boutonnieres

When you select flowers for your big day, find out what's in season during your wedding and what colors of blooms are available. For your bouquet (and your bridesmaids'), visit a florist and ask for his or her input, but be clear about the decade of your vintage-style wedding. A particular type of flower may not make or break your bouquet budget, but selecting a bloom that your mother or grandmother might have carried represents a nod to those important to you while also reinforcing your theme. Some popular

blooms that elicit nostalgia are cabbage roses, heirloom roses, carnations, peonies, ranunculus, delphiniums, dahlias, blush roses, stars-of-Bethlehem, airy fern fronds, and baby's breath, just to name a few.

If you want to spend your bouquet budget on flowers that won't fade (ever), go handmade! A custom brooch bouquet uses vintage-brooches instead of blooms, which means that your treasured heirlooms can be enjoyed both on your wedding day and forever after in a decorative vase. One place to browse vintage brooch bouquets is The Ritzy Rose, an online store which features some of the loveliest brooch bouquets I've ever seen.

If you can't decide between a floral or brooch bouquet, you can do both, using silver wire and a favorite brooch (or two). Wrap silver-colored jewelry wire (approximately 15" of wire per brooch) around the brooch multiple times to make a "stem." Stick the wire into your floral bouquet, and use wire cutters to snip the ends of the wire to fit. Wrap a flower handle or a ribbon around the stems and the wire (so you don't cut yourself). Or, an Art Deco forever bouquet can be created from lace, chiffon, glass pearls, and rhinestones. You might also consider a paper-flower bouquet.

If you opt for flowers, ivory and green are always an elegant combination; a vintage fabric wrap around the stems complements the bouquet beautifully.

You can create a bouquet handle by using a vintage handkerchief. Wrap it taut around the stems, then secure it with a pin. Accentuate the piece with a skeleton key or an antique spoon, which can be tied to the handle with a ribbon.

The groom's boutonniere can be as simple as a single floral bloom and greenery that coordinate with the bridal bouquet.

# The Reception

If your reception isn't within walking distance of the ceremony, ensure that guests know where to go by enclosing a map in each invitation (and be sure to have some maps on hand at the end of the ceremony to pass to guests as they leave). For a reception that takes place in the same venue, have a sign ready to guide guests to the party area.

Once guests arrive at your reception, greet them with cocktails, hors d'oeuvres, and personalized cocktail napkins, all located near your reception entrance.

## cocktail bar

Stock your bar with ingredients to make vintage cocktails, such as the Pimm's Rangoon, grasshopper, sloe gin fizz, passion royale, vodka gimlet, martini, Siboney, or Manhattan. Serve punch in a classic punch bowl, and as a finishing touch, serve cocktails in the appropriate vintage glassware. Offer bite-size appetizers like cocktail puffs, prosciutto-wrapped asparagus, canapés, or pinwheels.

## escort cards

If you're seating guests right away, and you've created table assignments, you'll need an escort-card display to show guests which table is theirs. An escort-card display can be as simple as tent cards — handwritten or printed from your computer — placed in alphabetical order or in a card holder on a small table.

Of course, there are other options that will suit your romantically vintage theme. Purchase a vintage typewriter on eBay or from a thrift store, and place it on a table with a sign that reads, "Find Your Table." In the typewriter, place a piece of paper with the table assignments and guests' names (typed in alphabetical order). A vintage suitcase can also become an escort-card display by propping open its case and stringing escort cards across the top.

Similarly, window panes can be used to show table assignments. Use white paint (try a chalk marker) to write table numbers and guests' names directly onto the glass.

If you're tying the knot at a winery, incorporate the atmosphere of the venue by using wine corks to hold your escort cards, see below. You can buy bulk quantities of natural, recycled wine corks online. Use an X-Acto knife to cut each cork in half lengthwise, so that it sits flat on your table; then cut a slit into each cork lengthwise, leaving a little room at the end. Insert your escort cards into the slits and place the corks, alphabetically, on a table at your reception entrance.

Another idea for an escort-card display with a nostalgic vibe is to use an old card catalog from a library. Label the outside of the drawers alphabetically, and place each escort card inside the appropriate drawer. Guests can step up to the catalog, open the drawer for their last name, and find the card with their table assignment.

For the escort cards themselves, look for "tea-stained" tags, luggage tags, or old-fashioned price tags. Embellish them further by tying a ribbon to each tag and adding a skeleton key.

Honey is one hand-decorated gift that is as sweet as can be. Embellish the containers with colorful twine and custom tags, and display a sign that invites guests to take a jar home and find their table.

## table numbers

A table number is required for guests to find their dining table. One of the easiest ways to display your table number is with a giant, painted clothespin. (You can find a natural-wood version at Factory Direct Craft, and simply apply a favorite paint.) The clothespin can stand up independently, or it can be clipped into your centerpiece arrangement.

Make your own table numbers by covering oversized wood numerals in Mod Podge and vintage fabric. The numbers can be propped up against your centerpiece.

## thank-you notes

At each dining table, you and your groom can add a handcrafted touch by displaying thank-you notes for guests, letting them know how much it means to you that they have joined the celebration of your marriage. A note at your guest's seat is also a perfect opportunity for including additional information about your reception.

## card box

A card box can be made from almost anything: an antique crate, an aged mailbox, or a vintage hatbox. Make sure that it's large enough to house all of the cards you will receive from your guests; you may need to use more than one container.

You can also search estate sales or resale shops for a vintage suitcase, which can be turned into a card box with a simple "Cards" sign attached. Make your own fabric sign with adhesive letters or paint, or string chipboard letters through a ribbon and tape the ends on either side of the suitcase.

## guest book

The guest book is an essential item that I believe should be used at every wedding. It is a keepsake for the bride and groom, with heartfelt messages and signatures from all guests in attendance.

The guest book has changed through the years, incorporating new ways to capture guests' sentiments. For instance, you could have guests sign a vintage hardcover novel or book of poetry, instead of signing a traditional journal-style guest book. Or, set up a typewriter (reminiscent of the era, of course!) on a table and instruct guests to type their names and well wishes onto paper (which can be framed and displayed in your home after the wedding).

One of my favorite guest-book ideas is interactive and makes a great icebreaker for guests. At each table, place a notebook that poses a question on the front, such as, "Where should we go for date night?" "What are your best marriage tips?" or "Where do you see us in 25 years?" Guests can fill out the book at their table and sign their names.

Another example of a vintage-inspired guest book that isn't a "book" at all is a set of customized "wish cards." Provide a stack of cards (simple card stock), or pieces of paper which have been adorned with a decorative stamp. Each guest can sign a card and write his or her wishes for the bride and groom. Guests can place their completed wish cards in antique bottles, a decorative box, or a tabletop tree (in this case, your cards will need a string attached for hanging).

To ensure that guests don't miss your guest book at your wedding, create a grand display. Incorporate a sign to show guests the location of the guest book, and include decorations to make the space pop.

## seating

At your head table or sweetheart table (a table for the bride and groom), make the chairs stand out with a pair of chair signs. You can create them yourself with card stock that matches your color palette, a paper hole punch, and ribbon. Or, visit a hardware store or home-improvement store and have two pieces of wood cut the same width as your chair backs. Use a drill to make a hole on either side of each wooden sign, and use ribbons to attach the sign to the chair back. Using a white paint pen (Sharpie makes one that works great), write "Mr." and "Mrs.," "Madame" and "Monsieur," your first names, or "Just" and "Married" on the signs. You can also cover the wood with chalkboard paint (Rust-Oleum offers an excellent paint-on version) and use chalk to inscribe your message. At the end of the wedding, you can erase the message and write "Thank" and "You" on the signs, take a photograph, and use it later on your thank-you cards. (Don't you just love multifunctional decor?) Another idea for stand-out seating is to borrow or rent two vintage chairs that are distinctly different from everyone else's.

If you're having a tented reception, incorporate vintage charm (and comfortable seating!) by setting up a small lounge area with antique couches, chairs, and a side table with flowers. Rent vintage furniture from a rental company that specializes in antique pieces, or borrow them from friends or family members with an eye for vintage style.

If you love vintage furniture — and your budget allows — purchase a piece or two for use at your reception. You'll have a beautiful seating area, and you can take the pieces home to enjoy after the big day.

If you'd like to add vintage decorations to your designated seating area, look for classic items like wire egg baskets, old keys, Mason jars, milk bottles and jugs, aged tin canisters, vintage hardcover books, antique mantel clocks, and milk-glass vases.

## centerpieces

The table centerpiece is one of the main focal points at a wedding reception. When guests enter the reception space, centerpieces are among the first accents they will see. For a clean, traditional look, cover each dining table with white linens and place a floral arrangement in the center.

Creating beautiful, vintage-style centerpieces is easy when you use the right components. Fill an old-fashioned teacup with flowers, place a glass vase with a floral bouquet nearby, incorporate vintage accents, and use Scrabble game tiles to spell out a wedding-related message.

Or, you could fill an antique pewter coffeepot or silver plated teapot with fresh flowers, or use a three-tiered dessert stand (with favors, treats, or flowers set on the plates) as a centerpiece.

In true vintage fashion, a patterned tablecloth — like the kind your grandmother may have used — can complement your color palette and add definition to your table arrangements.

A vintage birdcage — filled with flowers — makes a quaint and unexpected floral centerpiece. For added texture, place it on a table runner made of burlap.

For a classic table, use three basic pieces: a pop of color from your palette, a simple floral arrangement, and a vintage-inspired table number that guests can find easily.

A bottle of wine with a custom label and flower-filled bud vases become an elegantly old-fashioned centerpiece you can create yourself.

Centerpieces for your dinner tables, cake table, or card table can be as easy as floral arrangements with vintage tea pots, water pitchers, or glassware.

If a vase feels too conventional, showcase your flowers in vintage tea or coffee tins; honey buckets; cast-iron flower planters; rustic, tin flower baskets; or even small, antique jewelry chests with open drawers.

## favors

Wedding favors that are handmade are more meaningful; consider making your own to show guests your sincere appreciation.

I love when wedding favors are functional, since guests will have a reason to keep them long after the wedding is over. Some of my favorite treasured favors have been items that are useful in the home or office. For instance, a coffee mug is one of my favorite wedding favor ideas, particularly when it is are personalized. A personalized coffee mug (with the initial of each guest) makes an excellent escort card and wedding favor in one — simple add a tag with the guest's name and table number. Find these mugs at Anthropologie.

A muslin favor bag offers several options, because it's so versatile! Buy muslin spice bags, a stamp pad, and a vintage themed stamp (for example, a skeleton key). Add locally made candy; bags of flavored tea; small, decorative soaps; or lavender, which creates a drawer sachet. Stamp the bags, add your favors, and tie the drawstrings in a bow. Include a favor bag at each guest's place setting.

## the cake

Simple and sweet can't be beat! Place a cake on a vintage pedestal stand and add a custom topper of your choice. You can paint your own wooden cake toppers for under $10, using supplies from a craft store. You'll need wooden cake-topper dolls, acrylic paint, thin paintbrushes, a pencil, wood glue, and a round wooden base. (Since you don't want a painted surface to touch your cake, paint the wooden dolls and glue them onto the unpainted wooden base.)

Using your pencil, lightly sketch details onto the two wooden dolls: a dress, a bouquet of flowers, a necktie, a suit, faces, etc. Fill in the details with your paint. Allow the dolls to dry overnight, then use wood glue to attach the bottoms of the dolls to the wood base.

If you're not comfortable with drawing (or painting), you can leave this project to a professional, such as the Etsy stores Goose Grease or Knottingwood, two amazing resources for custom cake-topper dolls.

Another cake topper to consider is a simple wood or metal monogram, top left. Feeling crafty? Make a bunting-style cake topper from muslin fabric, cut into flags and strung from striped straws. Use a fine-point permanent marker to write your names or a simple phrase, such as "Just Married."

When serving cake, use an antique cake server and silverware, which you can keep after the wedding. Find vintage cake servers and silverware at flea markets or antique stores. You can get them hand stamped, too — try Wooden Hive for vintage silverware and custom stamping.

# entertainment

## GAMES

To underscore your vintage theme, set up tables in an area of your reception (outdoors, if the weather allows) and offer vintage board games for guests to play. Look online for vintage games from your particular decade of inspiration, like Scrabble, Battleship, or Life. If space for playing games isn't available, the board games can be used as a decorative accent instead.

## PHOTO BOOTH

One of the easiest ways to get guests to interact (other than dancing) is with a photo booth. A properly constructed photo booth can highlight your theme and provide memorable snapshots for guests to take home.

First, you'll want to create a backdrop where guests will pose for their photos. You can use ribbons or a length of pretty, patterned fabric (like a vintage tablecloth) as a backdrop, or simply designate a photo-booth space against a decorative wall at your reception, and include a chair. Purchase plenty of vintage-themed photo-booth props, like hats, oversized sunglasses, boas, wigs, mustaches, and more, from any party-supply store. You can also make your own photo-booth props — use cardboard, construction paper, wooden dowels, and paint to make vintage-style top hats, red lips, mustaches, cigars, and martini glasses.

Place the props (and extra boxes of instant film) in a decorative container, set the instant camera in a prominent spot, use a sign to draw attention to your photo booth, and include instructions on how to operate the camera and print the photos. For an even easier experience, you could rent a real photo booth — the rental company will set up, take down, and operate the booth from start to finish.

Make sure your playlist or that of the deejay includes plenty of era-appropriate classics to dance to, like songs from Frank Sinatra, Andy Williams, Nat King Cole, Harry Belafonte, and Dean Martin. Include song-request cards at each table, so that guests can ask for their favorite "oldies." Or, hire big band-style musicians to play covers of classic crooners.

## send-off

Make your grand exit at the end of the reception, with a vintage car waiting to pick you up! Search online for a company that rents classic vehicles, such as a vintage Rolls-Royce, Cadillac limousine, or Packard limousine. Don't forget to have a "Just Married" banner attached to the back for the ultimate getaway picture.

# Resources

Page 17

Pistachio Press / www.pistachiopress.com;
Ello There / www.etsy.com/shop/ElloThere;
Jen Simpson Design / www.jensimpsondesign.com

Page 19

Jen Simpson Design / www.jensimpsondesign.com;
Amanda Day Rose / www.amandadayrose.com;
Zazzle / www.zazzle.com;
United States Postal Service / www.usps.com;
Kenmore Stamp / www.kenmorestamp.com;
Champion Stamp / www.championstamp.com;
eBay / www.ebay.com

Page 25

Minature Rhino / www.etsy.com/shop/MiniatureRhino

Page 28

eBay / www.eBay.com;
Etsy / etsy.com;
BHLDN / www.BHLDN.com;
Ruche / www.ShopRuche.com

Page 30

Emici Bridal / www.Emicibridal.com

Page 34

Fleet Collection / www.fleetcollection.com;
ModCloth / www.modcloth.com

page 37

The Ritzy Rose / www.TheRitzyRose.com

Page 43

Factory Direct Craft / www.factorydirectcraft.com

Page 49

Anthropologie / www.anthropologie.com

Page 50

Goose Grease / www.etsy.com/shop/goosegrease;
Knottingwood / www.etsy.com/shop/KnottingWood;
Wooden Hive / www.etsy.com/shop/WoodenHive

# Farmhouse Rustic

While I am crazy about wedding themes of all kinds, the farmhouse theme has positively stolen my little handmade heart. This theme is rustic homespun goodness at its finest, right in the heart of an amazing backdrop: Mother Nature herself. In this chapter, I'll shower you with handcrafted ideas for a wedding on a farm, in a field, or in the woods — or a Western style complete with cowboy boots. I'll share some of my favorite handcrafted items, and provide you with pointers on how to make your wedding fun, memorable, and comfortable for you and your guests.

# Invitations & More

Once you've set a date, it's time to announce the exciting news to family and friends. Many couples opt for a "suite" of invitations. A suite carries a stationery design from beginning to end, and you can have as many pieces or as few as you want, even if you're making them all yourself.

## save the dates & invitations

A save-the-date card is sent to your guests early on, and it sets the tone for your big day. The card is the invitation's sidekick: it doesn't give away the punch line, but it clues the audience in to the main event. It presents just the bare essentials: who is getting married, when, and where. (For location, keep mum on the venue — only reveal the city and state/country at this time.) As a general rule, the save the date should never shine brighter than the invitation, so keep it simple. Mail the card four to six months before the event, especially if yours will be a destination wedding.

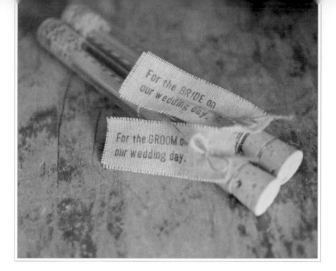

The invitations are the main event, and they can range from a set of three items (an invitation and envelope, a reception card, and a response card with an envelope) to a dozen themed pieces that might include a direction card, a map, a rehearsal invitation, and more. The mini-suite, opposite, from Amanda Day Rose is printed on a wood-grain-like paper with the same pattern as the envelope liner. A special addition to your suite could be these sweet "vials" of love, above, from Wood & Grain which contain notes to be delivered to the bride and groom before the ceremony. I always love to come across couples who find unique ways to personalize their wedding and in this section, you'll see examples of how a farmhouse-rustic theme can be communicated in your wedding stationery.

## make your own invitations

If your talent lies in illustration or graphic design, why not create your own artwork and layouts? Look for theme-appropriate paper and embellishments in an art-supply shop or craft store. Add an accent like twine, hemp cord, or linen ribbon. Make your own envelope seals with kraft-paper stickers. At your local office-supply store, you can find packs of kraft-paper stickers (by Avery), which include a template for printing right at home. If you have time, learn how to make 3-D cards, pop-up cards, or die cuts featuring your motif.

## custom invitations

Making your own wedding stationery can be a big task to take on yourself, especially if you don't have the time or the inclination — but you don't have to go it alone! Search online for designers, visit online stores like Etsy, or check my site, EmmalineBride.com, for vendors. One huge benefit to ordering handmade stationery is the ability to speak with the designer directly, often leaving plenty of room for a customized invite. Share

your vision with him or her, include inspiration found from your venue, and be specific about what you want. Together, you can create an entirely memorable, original design.

Guests love to see a visual of the happy couple, so include a photograph from your engagement (or a favorite moment in your courtship) as part of your invitation suite.

## CHOOSING A COLOR PALETTE

The colors you choose will work hand in hand with your motif and help to carry your theme. Rustic-farmhouse weddings lean towards neutral, nature-inspired hues of green, beige, and brown (as with this invitation, right, from Amanda Day Rose), with an emphasis on bright color in the summer and gold and orange in the fall — but choose what works

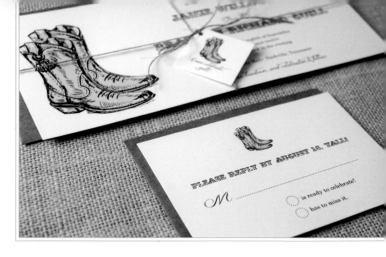

for you. Like any details you decide to use for your wedding, a color palette can be used in many areas, including bouquets, reception decor, colorful accents for the wedding party's attire, and even the frosting on your wedding cake. You can also take inspiration from the other areas of your wedding as you plan and design your wedding stationery.

## CHOOSING A MOTIF

The secret to a themed save-the-date card, invitation suite, and more is a cohesive palette, as described above, and an emblematic motif that represents you as a couple.

One of my favorite rustic-wedding motifs is a red barn. A barn is the classic icon of country life. If you're thinking, "How can that represent us as a couple?" consider instead what a red barn represents to *you*. For us, a red barn is a model of Americana. A farm, a small town, and fields of wheat or sunflowers all embody what we, as a couple, are about — where we want to plant our roots and enjoy the simple things in life. The same red barn might remind you of the countryside, your love for visiting the local farmers market every Saturday in July, or antiquing at local "barn sales" and flea markets. Perhaps it's the architecture you find charming. Maybe a red barn is your wedding location and the beginning of your new life together. In many ways, a motif — in our case, a barn — is never just an object.

Similarly, a tree — another motif — is never just a tree. A tree gets stronger with age, just as relationships do. Your courtship could be represented by a sapling, growing in fresh soil. Over time, strong roots take hold and your relationship grows, as does the image of the tree.

Some other examples of rustic motifs include wildflowers, leaves, mountains, the woods, horses, birds, deer, antlers, mason jars, hay bales, a farmhouse, horseshoes, and Western-style cowboy boots. Not sure which direction to go? Borrow an element from your venue. Marrying in the woods? Look for an invitation with oak trees or a tree "carving" with your initials. When you incorporate a venue-inspired element into your design, the result is a more personal and memorable invitation.

Are you planning a Western-style wedding on a ranch, farm, or in a barn? Use cowboy boots, as in this suite from Amanda Day Rose above, as a motif in your invitations.

The design of your invitation and the type of materials used are supporting elements

to the theme. Look for invitations made from kraft-paper card stock, wildly popular due to its natural feel. The save-the-date card and invitation from Wood & Grain, above left and right, are perfect for a farmhouse wedding. Ivory or cream card stock are also fitting, especially when paired with jute twine, hemp, or linen string tied around the center.

I've seen more bicycle-inspired invitations, save-the-date cards, and enclosures than I can count, as well as bicycles used as props in engagement photos and as "getaway" vehicles at weddings. Most often you'll find a tandem bicycle, (as in this design, below, from Jen Simpson Design), which symbolizes two people pedaling together as one — an especially fitting image for a wedding.

One of my favorite alternatives to a nature-inspired motif is a custom portrait or illustration of the couple. Since a rustic wedding is more informal, this invitation style works well.

To begin your search, I recommend browsing stationery shops or online. There are so many incredibly talented small businesses that would love to help you create the perfect invitation. For this theme, you'll want to search keywords such as "rustic" wedding invitations, "farmhouse" save the dates, and "woodland," "wood grain," or "barn wedding" invitations. If you have a custom design in mind, just ask — many artisans are happy to work with you on a special order.

# The Ceremony

Where do you dream of making your commitment to each other? Underneath a sycamore tree in the woods? In a beautifully decorated barn, decked out with miniature white lights? Or, do you envision walking through a field to a spot where you and your honey will be married under a handmade canopy on a gorgeous summer's day? Would you like a rustic farmhouse in the picture — a place where you can get dressed with your bridesmaids? Where would you like your guests to gather for the ceremony? How will you let them know where it is? What will you do with the seating and aisle decor? Once you pin down your desires and find a location, you'll find that dozens of details will fall right into place.

## tips on selecting a rustic venue

Finding your perfect rustic venue is easier when you know where to look. Suppose you live in a bustling big city, but you dream of tying the knot in a farmhouse setting. Solution: Don't limit yourself to your own backyard. Search the Internet for rustic wedding locations and find one within your home state — or expand even farther and go wherever your search takes you. I recommend places that specialize in weddings, because they will be equipped for necessities (like electrical outlets, tables, chairs, a kitchen, restroom facilities, and maybe even linens).

If you want to get married in a woodland setting, but you don't know where to start looking, consider national parks. While tying the knot anywhere in the woods sounds really easy (and insanely affordable), it's a whole lot trickier once you add guests. You want to be considerate of those in attendance, so details like comfortable seating, well-maintained grounds, restroom facilities, even terrain, and parking are just a few of the things to think about. National parks will have all of the above — some even have contracts with caterers who will come on-site. Plus, many have covered facilities for a reception or in case of inclement weather (a must-have to include in your backup plan!). You'll need to obtain a permit to rent an area in the park, and rules will vary by location.

For a list of national parks near you and for details, visit the National Park Service online.

If a national park isn't nearby, or you'd prefer a more homemade touch, consider having a backyard wedding — you'll get a homespun feel without the look of a typical backyard party. If you don't have a backyard, maybe you can arrange to "rent" one from

a friend or family member. Know what you want and agree to terms beforehand, such as how much you'll pay (if anything), the date, the duration, electrical requirements, restroom facilities, and if there are places that are off-limits to guests. Keep in mind that you'll need to take care of many details yourself, like rentals, linens, electrical, and more, but if you're up for the challenge, the result can be truly memorable.

Many couples share a dilemma about the location: you want to have your wedding in a spot with a rustic flair, such as a barn, but you both wish to marry in a place of worship. This one's easy! It doesn't have to be all or nothing; simply recite your vows in your place of worship and follow up with a reception in the most elaborately rustic venue you can find. Just keep in mind that you'll have to arrange transportation to the reception.

It goes with the territory that there is always the chance of inclement weather. Don't let unpredictable skies ruin your day — plan ahead, and have a tent set up or an indoor facility rented, just in case. If your venue location is in a rainy part of the world, provide umbrellas, rain ponchos, or rubber boots (in lots of different sizes!) for your guests.

Finally, sometimes tying the knot at an unconventional location — a barn, a forested area, or a park — can be baffling to those who may not understand your vision. "Back in the day," tying the knot in a barn or in the woods may not have seemed the slightest bit romantic, but today these settings are completely acceptable — and, actually, quite popular. Remind yourselves that it's your wedding day, and be true to the dreams of both of you. Besides, once your guests arrive and see how completely and utterly gorgeous your wedding is, you'll be reminded of the perfection of your choice. Furthermore, it will be a reflection of you as a couple, which is most important anyway.

## decor

When you are planning a farmhouse wedding, sometimes the ceremony location will be more than just a few steps away from where guests will park. It is important, then, to show guests where the wedding will be held, and this can be done in a decorative and fun way. I love these simple, do-it-yourself signs constructed from wood and white paint, this page and opposite.

A rustic wedding is more casual, which means that seating should follow suit. An emerging trend for rustic weddings — and all weddings, really — is to toss the convention of the bride's family seated on one side and the groom's on the other. Since it is a celebration of two people joining together in unity — and two families becoming one — many couples are letting guests know that there are no restrictions for seating at their ceremony.

The first decision to tackle is your focal point, the area where you'll exchange vows. The focal point should be in a central location with enough room for your guests, your chairs, and an aisle. A proper focal point will define and formalize your space.

For a traditional (and often indoor) ceremony, your focal point is most likely already established, such as an altar or chuppah. For an unconventional venue like a barn, farm, field, or the woods, a backdrop or other constructed piece is perfect for adding a touch of formality.

An arch, arbor, or pergola made from plain wood beams; wrought iron draped with lengths of grapevine; or a stack of reclaimed logs are "natural" choices for a ceremony

backdrop. If making your own is out of the question, you can always rent an arbor or arch from a rental company, which means that you'll also enjoy the benefits of having it set up and taken down for you. For a simple wood arch, use two tall wooden fence posts, with metal post supports on either side and one piece of wood nailed across the top. If you'd like to soften its rough-hewn look, there's lots of options to consider. You could hang lengths of muslin from the top portion so that they fall softly to the ground. Or try a vine-covered arch with grapevines, eucalyptus branches, olive branches, or create a magnolia

garland (make your own, or find faux garlands easily online). Sola flowers, made from a tapioca plant, can decorate anything from your cake to an arbor. Learn to make them yourself, or look on Etsy or try sites such as Roxy Heart Vintage.

Instead of using an arch or arbor, you could work with what is already in place. Is your ceremony in the woods? Pick a large tree as your focal point and backdrop. For a handmade touch, create a photo "wall" on your tree using twine. Tie one end of the twine to a branch, wrap the twine tightly around the tree, knot the end, and use a stake to secure it into the ground. On the twine, use clothespins to attach photographs of you and your fiancé (collected from friends and family) or include cards with favorite quotes, song lyrics, or other meaningful works with which you identify.

Planning a barn wedding? A barn itself is charming, so why not make it work as a backdrop? Arrange ceremony chairs to face the front. Allow extra room for you, your groom, and the officiant to stand. The wall of the barn can be left as is, or you can hang colorful banners, seasonal wreaths, or heart-shaped paper garlands across the wall. Hanging lengths of ribbon or bundles of herbs, sunflowers, or wildflowers will also brighten up a barn.

If the location you've decided upon has a built-in backdrop of breathtaking scenery, then you are all set. Any additions should be minimal, to allow the natural beauty to shine.

The key to a well-defined ceremony space is a decorated aisle. Here are a few easy ways to make yours stand out.

Clear glass vases filled with (battery-operated) candles can be placed atop tree stumps along the aisle. You don't need a tree-stump candle display at the end of every aisle, just a few to create a warm ambiance. Wondering where to find some tree stumps? Search in your local area, or call tree-cutting services, landfills, local parks departments, and lumber mills. As a side note, be careful where you pick up tree stumps; some have bugs like termites or beetles, and it's best to not transfer them to your ceremony space. Other options include wooden crates, large tree slices, or tree slabs, which are easy to purchase online. As a guide, use a tree slice that is 11"–15" in diameter.

For a do-it-yourself outdoor project, create a whimsical heart-lined aisle. Attach simple wood hearts (available at craft stores) to wood dowels or twigs, using hot glue. When dry, display the hearts along the sides of your aisle by placing them firmly into the ground. You can paint the hearts to coordinate with your decor or leave them natural.

Poems, lyrics from songs, Biblical passages or meaningful quotes can be turned into rustic decor. Print any of the above on a piece of card stock, punch a hole at the top, and string a ribbon through the hole. Hang the signs from pews or benches along the aisleway.

Incorporate seasonal fruits or vegetables into your aisle decor, for a pop of color and an at-home feel. For example, use small gourds or pumpkins in small stacks to decorate the aisle. Bushel baskets filled with apples or peaches look great at the entrance of your aisle or your focal point, especially when placed atop hay bales. Or, use what's in nature around you to decorate the aisle; sprinkle freshly fallen leaves in the autumn, or infuse the aisle with sprigs of fresh lavender or rose petals and rosemary in the spring or summer.

*The Ceremony*/Farmhouse Rustic **67**

Rustic, weathered birdcages are some of my favorite decor pieces — they're so versatile. A birdcage, which typically has a hook on top, can be filled with fresh flowers or candles and displayed from shepherd's hooks lining the aisle.

You could also place potted plants (or a large arrangement of baby's breath) in a burlap bag, or wrap the bottom in linen or burlap fabric. To wrap it yourself, place a sheet of natural burlap underneath the potted plant and gather the sides upwards around the pot. Wrap moss wire or preserved floral-wire twine around the center to form a bow. Place the plants along the sides of the aisle.

Make a statement with a dramatic arrangement inside a tall galvanized pail. Items like corn stalks, manzanita branches, willow branches, or cotton branches with raw cotton are just a few accent ideas.

## AISLE RUNNER

An aisle runner will define your aisle, whether indoors or out. A burlap aisle runner can pull together a rustic look. You can make your own, using a roll of burlap from a craft store. If you're outdoors, roll it out and use stakes to attach it firmly to the ground. If you're indoors, a linen aisle runner may be best, since burlap tends to shed and can be uneven unless it's pulled taut and staked into the ground. Linen will also coordinate with your rustic look, plus it's easy to embellish with large monogrammed stencils and acrylic paint to make it your own.

As a side note, I advise wearing ballet flats or sandals down the aisle if you will be using a burlap aisle runner, as its texture may cause it to get snagged on heels. Instead of an aisle runner, let petals, sunflowers, wildflowers, or herbs decorate the sides of your aisle, so your ground (preferably grass) makes its own visual "aisle."

## seating

Now that you've given some thought to your decor, let's talk about seating. How will your guests be seated at your ceremony?

If you're getting married in a place of worship, chairs (usually pews or benches) will be provided, so you won't need to plan ahead for seating. In an outdoor or indoor setting without established seats, you may have to provide your own. The most popular ceremony seat is a standard chair, typically a white plastic or metal folding chair, or a hardwood specialty chair (like Chiavari). Find a rental company and preview their chairs, either in person or online. Depending on your venue (and the terms you agree upon with the rental company), chairs will be delivered, set up, and removed from the premises for you. This means a stress-free experience and a pulled-together look, all with the help of a professional company.

A popular seating choice for rustic weddings is the hay bale, a farming-staple-turned-seating-option. Hay bales allow guests to sit comfortably, while their unique look contributes to your rustic vibe. However, there are a few faux pas to avoid when using hay bales as seating. First, make sure there are enough bales to accommodate all guests. Depending upon the size of the bales you buy, only a couple of guests can sit on each one. It's better to have too many seats than not enough. Second, you should always cover the tops of the hay bales. Guests will be dressed up, and hay sticks to clothing very easily. Also, hay can be extremely itchy (especially for women wearing dresses or skirts), so covering the bale will make the seat more comfortable. There are many ways to cover hay bales, but my favorite (and the easiest) is with flat bed sheets. Visit a thrift store to buy (gently used) flat sheets and wash them well. For a pulled-together look, wrap the top of a hay bale with a sheet and pull the ends on either side together with a simple knot of ivory or burlap ribbon. Alternatively, you could cover the hay bales with patchwork quilts, vintage tablecloths, or wide pieces of linen fabric, measured to fit.

Your ceremony is falling right into place: your location is set, the decor is looking good, and your guests will be seated comfortably. Let's move on to some specific ceremony decor tips and helpful extras that you may wish to incorporate.

## ceremony program

While not a requirement, a ceremony program is one detail that can make a terrific keepsake of your ceremony. The program keeps a record of your readings, songs you've selected, and special traditions followed; some couples even include their vows. It also introduces guests to your wedding party and outlines different parts of the ceremony. For this type of wedding, look for a program that is printed on faux wood or a tined card stock with a natural feel. A bonus is that it can double as a fan in case of hot weather. Informal programs fit right in to this theme, so feel free to enclose pennant banners that say "Hooray" for waving when the bride and groom walk down the aisle, or packets of confetti or seeds for tossing. Place programs in a large wooden box, galvanized pail, crate, or wire basket, so guests can pick one up as the enter the ceremony space. The container can be reused as a wedding-card box at your reception.

### VOWS

If you'll be reciting your own vows, you will need a place to hold the written copies. A wooden cigar box can make a fantastic, lightweight vow box. For an easy project you can tackle at home, gather the following from a craft store: a wooden box with a clasp, white acrylic paint, a pack of lettering stencils, and a stencil brush. Use the paint, stencil brush, and stencils to display the wedding date and both of your initials, or write "Vows" across the top. Allow it to dry overnight.

A small, blank journal can serve as a vow book (or find custom-made vow books on Etsy). For a rustic vibe, look for a book or journal with a faux birch-bark or wooden cover. The vow box or book can be carried down the aisle by a "vow bearer," an attendant the same age as your flower girl or ring bearer. The book or box can be placed on a designated table until it's time to exchange vows.

## flower girl & ring bearer

One of the stars of the show — the flower girl — will need a basket to hold her petals for tossing. Two of my favorite examples are moss-covered and birch-bark-wrapped baskets, like this one on the top right from PNZ Designs, which reflects the theme beautifully. Look for a small galvanized pail, which can be personalized with a wooden heart or wooden luggage tag tied around the handle with a ribbon. Use a wood-burning tool to inscribe her name. A simple silk flower, with its stem wrapped around the handle, makes the flower basket even cuter, which means she'll really want to carry it. Other baskets include wicker, grapevine, wire, or wood.

The flower girl doesn't have to toss petals or carry a basket. Some alternatives include a wooden sign or pennant flag that reads, "Here Comes the Bride;" a wand made of wood, and decorated with felt, ribbons, or streamers; and a moss-covered pomander attached to a ribbon and filled with lavender or a favorite herb.

For the ring bearer, look for a ring pillow made from burlap and covered in lace or adorned with a linen flower. A tree slice can be converted into a ring "pillow" — just use a wood-burning tool to personalize it with your wedding date or monogram. Wrap a sturdy piece of twine around the slice and attach the rings. A ring box is a favorite alternative, since you don't need to worry about the rings falling to the ground (they're kept safely inside). Craft stores sell small, unfinished wood boxes, complete with hinges and a latch. Use paint or stain to coat the outside of the box; use a wood-burning tool to personalize the top with "Rings," "I Do," or "Mr and Mrs." Line the inside of the box with standard craft felt, or fill it with moss.

A well-aged horseshoe is my favorite offbeat ring "pillow." It can be such a fitting accent, with its vintage patina and outdoor aesthetic — and it's a symbol of good luck. To attach your rings, just take a piece of string or ribbon and knot one end to the horseshoe; thread your rings through and knot the other end securely.

A ring pillow doesn't have to be purchased; some of the best ring pillows are free. One benefit of a rustic wedding is that nature is right at your fingertips. Unexpected — but functional — ring-pillow alternatives can be found outside; all you need to do is attach a piece of twine to secure your rings. Examples include a small stack of twine-wrapped twigs; a large pine cone; an apple, pumpkin, or gourd, depending on the season. Another "free" item, which you may already have in your possession, is a vintage, weathered book, preferably one that's meaningful to you.

## wedding-party gifts

A gift is a special token of thanks and appreciation for members of your wedding party. The best time to present gifts is before the ceremony.

For groomsmen, look for organic, reusable items. A set of wood-grain cuff links, a handmade wood-backed journal, personalized tree-slice coasters, a reclaimed-wood charging station, an antique cast-iron wall-mount bottle opener, a leather-wrapped flask, or an engraved cigar box with cigars, a cigar cutter, and a lighter inside are all great ideas. Cigar boxes filled with beer soap, leather shaving bags, or rustic leather wallets are also gifts that your groomsmen would be happy to receive.

For bridesmaids, focus on natural, functional gifts as well. Some ideas include handmade soaps, a linen-and-lace clutch or tote, an engraved wooden jewelry box, a wood-grain-inspired ring dish, a leaf-shaped pendant necklace or earrings, check out Little Hunny Studio on Etsy.

If your wedding is country themed, give your ring bearer a cowboy hat and a sheriff-style wooden badge pin that is engraved with "Ring Bearer." Or, give him an engraved box filled with toy cars.

The flower girl would love a special jewelry box filled with a necklace, bracelet, or set of earrings. A wooden frame personalized with her — with her name in which a wedding-day photograph can be placed later — also makes a beautiful keepsake gift.

# The Attire

As I mentioned previously, a rustic wedding leans more to the casual than the formal. As a result, there are so many fun options for attire for the bride, the groom, and the wedding party that it can be hard to choose. But choose you must. I'm never at a loss to suggest handcrafted touches, and in this chapter, I won't let you down. You'll find plenty of ways to add your own flair, from discovering unexpected places to use your color palette to fabric suggestions and even hairstyle ideas.

## the bride

What type of wedding dress do you think of for a farmhouse-chic wedding? My ideal approach is to think about contrasts. For example: pair a linen slip dress with a gauzy, chiffon bolero jacket, or a silk-charmeuse waisted gown with a colorful screen-printed sash, or maybe a vintage beaded top with a fabulous denim floor-length skirt. If you're marrying in the woods or literally on a farm, a dress without a train is a smart choice — that train could get pretty dirty. There's no set rustic-gown look that you have to ascribe to — almost any style works with this theme.

A wedding veil is always a classic look, but it is not the only option available. One of the most stunning alternatives is a hair crown, also known as a hair wreath. A hair crown is usually handcrafted from organic, natural materials, such as grapevine or twine. It is also accented with elements like faux berries, Spanish moss, dried or fresh flowers, ferns, moss, or cotton.

HAIRSTYLES

While a braid may sound like an overly casual hairstyle, it is perfectly appropriate within the rustic realm. Unlike other themes, a rustic theme is natural, not fussy. A less polished hairstyle, such as a informal braid or a casual topknot, fits right in.

A side braid can be given a more tousled appearance by loosening the braid with the open end of a bobby pin; wispy, sideswept bangs finish the look.

Achieve the effect of a hair crown by braiding your hair into a wreath shape. This style lasts from ceremony to reception and holds up well to heat and humidity, provided you also have plenty of bobby pins and hair spray in place.

A waterfall braid is the perfect mix of an elegant and rustic look. It can be achieved by separating your hair into three sections. Begin by French braiding one section starting at the temple. As you cross the top strand over the first section, drop the strand and pull a new strand underneath from the opposite side. (There are fantastic how-to tutorials online — try YouTube). This style is easier than it sounds, especially if you've already mastered the French braid, and works best for medium to long wavy locks.

For shorter hair, add soft waves first to give your hair texture. Put one small section of hair into a thin braid; then pull the braid over your head like a headband for a halo-like, bohemian look.

## SHOES

Once you've selected the perfect dress, hairstyle, handcrafted accessories, and jewelry, you're ready to pick out shoes to match. In my perfect world of rustic chic, the bride, groom, and wedding party would be fashionably decked out in cowboy and cowgirl boots. However, I know that you may not live in the country, you may not own a pair of Western-style boots, and ten of your closest friends may also not have a pair of boots ready to wear. In such cases, the next best thing (in everyone's closet already) is a pair of brown dress shoes or loafers for the men. The women are best outfitted in a pair of flats or sandals that can handle uneven terrain like grass or dirt. Vegan flats, which are handmade from natural organic cotton or burlap, are also available look at New Bride Co.

## JEWELRY

Even your jewelry — including your wedding ring — can exude a rustic flair. Look for a nature-inspired wedding band, such as one that looks like a twig. One of my favorites is from jewelry designer Kristin Coffin, below right; it features scattered diamonds embedded on a decorative gold band. If you're wearing a necklace with your gown, remember to choose a piece that is meaningful to you. A favorite element from nature — an acorn charm, "engraved" wooden heart charm, or leaf charm — are a few examples that can remind you of your first date (did you go hiking?) on your wedding day.

## the groom

The groom can dress in attire that makes him feel comfortable, yet stylish and pulled together. A few ideas include a dress shirt and khaki pants, paired with oxfords; or a plaid button-down shirt and jeans, paired with Western boots. Look for layering pieces, like a vest worn over a button-down shirt, or suspenders paired with a bow tie and worn with casual pants. The groom can enhance his attire (and set himself apart from the groomsmen) with an accent piece, such as a unique boutonniere or a bow tie that differs just slightly from the groomsmen's.

## wedding party

Once the bride's and groom's attire is finalized, it's time to create a look for the wedding party. Begin by considering your color palette and any design motifs you may have selected for invitations and decor.

The palette can be as bright or neutral as you desire, but it is important to remain consistent once you have decided on a particular shade. Select a tone for bridesmaids to wear, and have them choose their own dresses to suit their individual shape. Or, you could go the traditional route and select a dress for each bridesmaid. In this setting, members of the wedding party could wear flats, sandals, sneakers, or boots (or match the bride's footwear). Comfortable shoes complement this theme famously.

### BRIDESMAIDS

Handcrafted weddings are all about harnessing creative and unconventional approaches, and the bridesmaid's attire is no exception. Avoid the traditional bridesmaid-dress dilemma by allowing your bridesmaids to choose any dress they wish. For a tailored look, limit the dress selection to a particular shade and length, they can decide on the dress that flatters them best, and they'll absolutely want to wear it again.

## GROOMSMEN

The groomsmen can have a lot of fun with this wedding theme. A dark gray shirt, a pair of suspenders, dark pants or jeans, and maybe even a bow tie in a muted color — alongside the groom's light-gray summer-weight suit — would be picture perfect. A pair of khaki pants, paired with a pale green or even pink shirt and a skinny tie, is another option. A small-checked or plaid shirt, a linen vest, striped socks, a lightweight newsboy hat and boots, sneakers, or even oxfords — with color-coordinated shoelaces — are all fair game. A suit is not out of the question.

## RING BEARER & FLOWER GIRL

The ring bearer is best suited in a miniature version of the groomsmen's attire. This can be a classic suit and tie, or a casual button-down shirt, a pair of suspenders, and a bow tie. Western boots are a plus, especially if the groomsmen are outfitted in them, too.

For your favorite little girl, find a flower-girl dress in a comfortable, breathable, and washable natural fabric. Add a decorative sash or a puffy slip underneath to provide a fantasy quality to her dress. Make sure it's "spinnable," so she can twirl and curtsey. Give her a really cute purse and hair accessory, as well as a light wrap in case it's cool.

# The Flowers

Floral decor can be a feast for the eyes, whether it includes blooms from your garden or woodland arrangements. Consider a range of summer favorites, if that's when your celebration will be: lavender, stems of rosemary, eucalyptus, and other herbs paired with daisies, purple veronica, sage, amaranthus, sunflowers, and a world of wildflowers. Even vegetables can play a part, as table decor or as components in a wreath or garland.

## bouquets & boutonnieres

What kind of flowers will you carry? Be on the lookout for blossoms that exude a casual, woodland feel, with greenery added for texture. A few decorative varieties are garden roses, anemones, sage, silver brunias, bear grass, dusty millers, and scabiosa pods. As an offbeat option, consider a bouquet created from dried wheat or baby's breath, which looks surprisingly chic when carried down the aisle. Wrap the stems in vintage lace for a finishing touch.

Dried-flower bouquets fit in beautifully with a rustic wedding — and they last a long time. Look for bouquets made from sola flowers in the shapes of shells, carnations, or mums, accented with greenery or baby's breath. Some unconventional alternatives include a bouquet made entirely from pinecones, felt flowers, birch-wood roses, or handmade lace flowers accented with feathers. Make your own bouquet, using an eclectic assortment of wildflowers, and add items from the forest — moss, berries, and lichen — as accents.

To accessorize your wedding bouquet (and bridesmaid bouquets), wrap the stems to create a homemade handle. Use rope or cotton-muslin fabric in your accent color, wrap it taut around the stems, and secure it with natural jute twine tied in a knotted bow.

Once you've selected your flower bouquet, borrow an accent from it for your boutonnieres — like succulents, for example.

### BOUTONNIERES

Much like the attire, the boutonniere takes its cue from the bridal bouquet. Typically, it uses a single blossom — usually a stem of greenery from the bouquet — paired with a subtle accent. The boutonniere pictured (below, right) is a single succulent with a small twig and a leaf from a dusty miller plant, wrapped with twine and attached to the left side of the groom's or groomsmen's shirt, vest, or jacket lapel. A corsage is similar in that it contains those elements, but it often includes two or three blossoms plus accents. The corsage is also attached on the upper left side or worn on the left wrist.

For a handcrafted alternative, use a rosette made from fabric (such as linen, burlap, or cotton). Form a stem by wrapping a twig in ribbon, and accent it with a lace "leaf." This design works well in any season and can become a keepsake.

# The Reception

A farmhouse wedding inspires loads of creative ideas for a reception. Ideally, the festivities will take place in a barn, on a farm, or in the woods. But if you can't find the right place, or if a venue is out of your price range, you can still achieve a rustic look by placing the right accents throughout. Your selected reception site will play a large role in expressing your overall theme, beginning with the entryway. Make a memorable first impression on guests by incorporating decorative touches here and there throughout the reception space.

## cocktail hour

Following the ceremony, give guests a place to mingle, sip on beverages, and enjoy appetizers before the reception officially begins. Seating is not required here, but a few hay bales become an inviting place to relax before the party starts. Countrified cocktail tables can be crafted with 20" round glass tabletops set atop 18" whiskey

barrels. Skip the linen tablecloth here instead, the glass tabletops will put the spotlight on your austere whiskey barrels. Finish with an arrangement of fresh flowers inside a canning jar.

For your bar, include drinks that are easy for guests to grab themselves. Galvanized drink tubs can be filled with ice and bottles beer, root beer, soda, and water. Drink containers can be filled with iced tea, lemonade, punch, or a spiked drink. Label the dispensers clearly, and provide plenty of glasses or jars for guests to fill up. Pails filled with ice are perfect receptacles for bottles of bubbly at tables, along with glasses for toasting.

A rental company that specializes in vintage or antique furniture can help you achieve a rustic-chic seating area, using items like a pair of antique wooden chairs, an elegant sofa, and a coffee table. Bringing beautiful indoor-furniture pieces outdoors is a bit unconventional, but an offbeat sitting area will make the perfect mingling spot for guests.

The cocktail hour is a perfect opportunity for guests to try their hand at a few lawn games. Bocce ball, lawn darts, ladder ball, corn hole, horseshoes, and croquet are just a few of the games you can invite guests to play. Show guests where to go with a chalkboard sign  and set up the games away from the reception area.

## ESCORT CARDS

If you'd like guests to sit at specific tables, then escort cards are in your future. They show guests where to be seated, thus avoiding the problem of guests wandering the aisles looking for a place to sit. The cards can be as simple as prescored, lightweight card stock with names and table assignments handwritten or printed from your computer. Be sure to position the escort cards at the point where guests will be entering the area.

For a fun alternative to a traditional escort card, give guests an opportunity to get a drink and find their table at the same time by using mason-jar drinking glasses. You

can find pint-size mason jars, chalkboard tags with a prepunched hole, a chalk pen, and twine. You can find all of these supplies at any craft store — and mason jars are sold at grocery stores, though it is easier to buy bulk quantities online. Use your chalk pen to write the guest's name and table assignment onto the tag, string it through the twine, and tie it in a knot around the lid of the mason jar. Place the jars together in alphabetical order on a table — near the bar — and guests can grab a glass, fill it up, and find their seat.

Create an escort card "clothesline" outdoors with the help of two trees that are growing close together. Wrap the clothesline around one tree and knot it; pull the line across to the other tree and make another knot. On your now-suspended line, use clothespins to attach escort card tags or cards.

Indoors, you can use a clothesline and an old picture frame with the glass portion removed. Prop the frame up by attaching a piece of wood with hot glue, or use a tabletop easel. Tie a length of clothesline to both ends of the frame and knot it. Arrange your escort cards in alphabetical order across the line, using clothespins, and place the display on a table near the entrance.

A seating-chart sign created from a chalkboard is another way to direct guests to their tables. If you have good penmanship, use a fine-point chalk pen to write guests' names and table numbers on a large chalkboard. Arrange the names alphabetically, or, if you only have a handful of tables, arrange names underneath the appropriate table assignment. Prop the chalkboard sign against a potted plant or against the entryway of your reception.

A wrought-iron gate becomes an easy-to-display escort-card wall; simply attach escort-card tags with clothespins.

A wooden tray filled with a bed of artificial moss becomes a perfect setting onto which escort cards can be placed. Make your own cards from rectangular kraft-paper tags. Add an embellishment (a lace ribbon, a doily, or a lace sticker) on one side, and place the tags onto the moss. If you're getting married in the autumn, use miniature gourds as place-card holders. Simply print place cards from your computer and use a pin to attach each card.

If you're using paper escort cards, arranging them can be tricky; you want to make the display visible enough for guests to notice and easy for guests to find their names. If you're planning a woodland wedding, for instance, you can use a reclaimed-wood frame, twine, and mini clothespins to display paper escort cards. Make sure the cards are attached alphabetically.

An old window can be turned into a decorative seating chart by using a glass pen. Write directly onto the window pane, and arrange the names by table.

Create a chic, colorful ribbon backdrop that can also function as an escort-card display. Begin by knotting twine on either end of two poles, or across beams within your reception space. Knot ribbons from the twine, and use clothespins to attach escort cards to the ribbons.

Or, use moss to create a table runner for your escort-card table, and "plant" your escort cards by pinning them directly to the runner.

*The Inspired Wedding*

## TABLE NUMBERS

Table numbers are essential if you plan to have assigned seating for guests. Here are some fun, nontraditional ideas for making your table numbers stand out.

Papier-mâché or wooden numbers are excellent options for simple, easy-to-make table numbers. Available at most craft stores, these letters come in different sizes and can be painted or left unfinished. You can turn papier-mâché letters into metal look-alikes by using metallic spray paint, which will add shine and texture to your display.

Use patterned paper and a marker to turn a small wooden or zinc frame into an easy, self-standing table number. Cut out a piece of patterned paper to fit inside the frame; use your marker to write the number onto the paper. Place the paper inside the frame and display it on the appropriate table.

A piece of reclaimed wood is the perfect background for do-it-yourself table numbers, using black address numerals from a hardware store. Use a hammer and nails to attach the table numbers to the piece of wood. To display, prop it against your centerpiece.

A simple suggestion for table numbers is to adhere a vinyl number decal to a glass jar filled with flowers. Rustic table numbers don't need to be fancy — just functional.

There are so many unexpected supplies in your own backyard that can become wedding decor. (The beauty of a rustic wedding is how rough and rustic the touches can be — imperfection is welcome.) For example, my husband and I recently replaced our backyard privacy fence, swapping old, weathered and worn planks for new dogwood. Once we had a pile of planks in our backyard, I began to imagine the many projects that could be created from them. I made table numbers from 8" pieces of reclaimed wood (preferably dogwood or pine, weathered), using a paintbrush and acrylic paint. First, I tried stenciling — but the weathered wood made it impossible for the lines to look clean. Instead, I resorted to freehand: I dabbed my paintbrush in paint and drew a number onto each piece of wood. Allow them to dry overnight, and then prop the table numbers against your centerpiece. If you need pieces of wood, visit a lumberyard (where you may score a cheap price) and inquire about rough pieces of dogwood. The cost of paint and a paintbrush is minimal — I spent less than $4 to make a set of twenty table numbers, since the wood was readily available.

Some of the best wedding details are those that serve two functions like combining escort cards and drinking glasses. Similarly, consider combining your place cards and wedding favors, saving both time and table space. To turn any wedding favor into a place card, just add a name tag, and have that particular favor placed at the guest's seat.

For example, tie a name tag around the center of a potted plant. (Before the wedding, create a seating chart and group favors in boxes labeled with table numbers. This will make setup a breeze.)

The place card itself may not seem "rustic" enough, but the place-card holder certainly can be. Place-card holders may be made from reclaimed birch-branch rounds (with a slit carved into the top for a place card to sit), pinecones (with a metal picture holder attached), or small wooden picture frames, with the place card inside.

## decor

If your wedding reception takes place outdoors, there may not be a specific entryway; however, a decorated pergola or trellis can define the space. For an indoor venue, decorate the doors or an other architectural feature with a grapevine wreath, moss monogram letters, or a summery floral wreath.

For a grand entrance to your reception, hang large, billowy muslin curtains across the open doorway. Use rope as curtain tiebacks. If your curtains cannot be attached to rafters, use a pipe and drape kit instead. Buy muslin fabric from a craft store and use hem tape for a no-sew curtain. Stencil the fabric drape with your monogram, the date, or simple image of a pinecone, cowboy boots, or rustic hearts.

When it comes to decorating, proper lighting is key. Lighting can instantly warm a space and make it look festive. You can string lighted white paper lanterns or metal candle chandeliers (use battery-operated candles) from ceiling beams (see an array of lights and hanging-shade ideas online at Luna Bazaar). Hanging glass orbs (with battery-operated lights inside), globe lights, lighted willow branches, and lighted rope can make for a luminous and cozy space, whether indoors or outdoors. An ordinary grapevine chandelier pops when LED wrap lighting is added; hang the chandelier from tree branches or ceiling beams. On tables, create a soft glow with wax luminaries or battery-operated candles set inside canning jars, tree-branch candleholders, antique bottles, or mercury-glass candleholders, or atop 20" clear-glass dessert pedestal stands. Add dramatic lighting to your entryway with wicker-and-chicken-wire-basket lanterns and battery-pillar candles inside, hung from a 12" shepherd's hook.

To line pathways or the perimeter of your space outdoors, create mason-jar solar lanterns. These lanterns are perfect for areas where you don't want to monitor candles — plus, they utilize the sun to create light that will last all evening. I made mason-jar solar lanterns for my back patio, and they're perfect for lighting stairs or pathways. To create your own, use a pint-size regular-mouth mason jar (with a lid and rim) and a solar light (find them on clearance after the summer at big-box stores). Remove the stake portion from the solar light and the metal rim from the solar light itself by sliding it off. Take off the lid from your mason jar, insert the solar light into the top of the jar, and place the rim over the solar light to hold it in place. Spray paint the rim black to match the solar light. Charge it in the daylight; in the evening, you'll be surprised by how beautiful the light looks through the jar and how much illumination it really provides.

Make the most of your space, whether large or small, by utilizing every single area. Hang a banner or wooden letters from a tree branch to spell out "I Do" or "Love." Or,

wrap solar lights around the trunk for hassle-free lighting at night. Suspend colorful yarn balls from tree branches; begin making them by blowing up a balloon. Create a paste with a full bottle of glue, a half cup of corn starch, and a quarter cup of water. Stir. Dip the yarn in the paste and wrap the yarn around the balloon. Allow all of the yarn balls to dry overnight. Pop the balloons and use the string to hang your yarn balls from tree branches or rafters in a barn.

One of my favorite hanging garlands is made of sola flowers, which I've mentioned previously. Since they're lightweight, you can string them with a needle and thread to create a floating-flower effect, ideal for decorating a backdrop wall.

If you have old aluminum cans, don't recycle them just yet — use the cans to create hanging decor! Remove the label from each can and thoroughly clean the inside. Drill a hole on two sides of the can; knot a piece of clothesline on either side for hanging. Fill the cans with fresh flowers, and hang a few from tree branches.

Tissue-paper rosettes make a remarkable impression, yet they're incredibly easy (and inexpensive) to make. You'll need a pack of gift tissue or scrapbook paper and a stapler. To make a paper rosette, fold one sheet of paper accordion style; fold it in half and staple the ends together. Do this with two more sheets of paper; then, staple the three sections together. Use tape to adhere the paper rosette to a wall. Add more (and smaller rosettes, using less paper) in layers until the wall is full. Paper rosettes are also light enough to hang from the ceiling with string.

Make your own cheerful bunting with fabric remnant squares (found at any craft store), hot glued to ribbon or twine and displayed near your entryway. Hot glue fabric onto a light card stock to make a stiffer bunting, or let the cloth hang to gently blow in the wind. For a bohemian look that's also polished, insert lace into embroidery hoops. Use yarn to suspend them from tree branches or rafters, and stagger the heights.

## CENTERPIECES

I love how inventive rustic-wedding centerpieces are — I've never seen the same style of centerpiece used twice.  Here are a few of my favorite ideas to inspire your own unique look.

Use an old tray or reclaimed-wood picture frame (with backing) to create a low-profile centerpiece. Cut a piece of cardboard to fit the inner size of the tray of frame. Glue reindeer moss to it. Place small succulents on top of the moss and add any finishing touches, such as flower buds or small pinecones.

Birch bark is one rustic item that is easy to find and use for decoration. Take a walk

in the woods and look for fallen birch bark (never take birch bark from a live tree). There should be plenty on the ground. Find a big piece of birch bark, large enough to wrap around a vase. Soak the bark in water overnight to make it pliable. Measure the vase you want to wrap, and cut the bark to fit, leaving one inch of overlap room to ensure that your vase is hidden underneath. Apply hot glue to the outside of the vase, and wrap the bark around the vase. Use a rubber band to keep the birch bark firmly glued to the vase, allow it to dry overnight. Once the glue has set, fill the vase with water and add fresh flowers.

When setting your dinner tables, use informal table coverings, such as fringe-edged linen or artificial-moss table runners. Atop each runner, swap frilly vases for rustic receptacles like galvanized pails, mercury glass, or wooden crates filled with flowers. Moss- or lichen-covered branches can add to the center of your table, bringing a bit of the outdoors inside.

For an alternative to fabric or moss table runners, try wood instead. A thin plank of wood becomes a table runner when mercury-glass votive candles, mason-jar vases,

vintage hardcover books, or antique glass bottles are placed on top. For a fuller look, fill in any empty spaces with preserved boxwood garlands or add lighted branches for illumination.

A long wooden log can be repurposed as a candleholder. Find a log (at least 12" in length) that can lie flat on a table, preferably a hard wood with bark on the outside. Place the log on a smooth surface and mark Xs where you'd like the candles to go. Use

a drill and a 1½" Forstner bit to make holes for the candles. Remove any sawdust, and sand the area to make the holes smooth. Place battery-operated tea-light candles inside.

A birch-bark pail becomes a conversation piece when filled with flowers and "engraved" with your initials, using a wood-burning tool (or a wood-burning letter set, which makes engraving much easier for beginners).

Using a cloche — also known as a bell jar — is one of the easiest ways to put a treasure (or a collection of treasures) on display, and it doubles as a centerpiece focal point. A cloche can showcase succulents, flowers, a stack of vintage books, antique wooden spools, or objects found in nature, like moss-covered stones, pinecones, or feathers. Faux antlers also look lovely when placed underneath a cloche, set atop a wood slice, and accented with baby's breath.

A wooden window box or barn-wooden planter box makes an exceptional centerpiece container. Fill a planter box with a bed of Spanish moss and place cacti, succulents, and knockout roses on top. A wooden milk-bottle crate or wine-bottle crate can be a vessel for potted plants or pillar candles; place one in each crate slot.

When setting the tables, place fringe-edged linen napkins inside grapevine, wooden, or wicker napkin holders. Or, tie green moss-colored jute twine around the napkin and make a bow.

## guest book

To record signatures and well wishes from guests, you'll need a guest-book station at your reception. Add flair to your guest-book table with a twig pencil for signing.

Be on the lookout for a book that has a linen, kraft, birch-bark, or wooden cover. Some craft stores offer unfinished-wood books with a hinged cover and room for 12" x 12" pages to fit inside. This book is practically begging you to put your own stamp on it; personalize the front with paint and stencils or use a heat tool to engrave your initials or "Guest Book."

If you think a functional item or a piece of artwork would be a better fit, try a guest-book alternative instead of a book. For example, fill a planter box with pieces of slate, river stones or wooden hearts, hang tags, or puzzle pieces. Invite guests to take one, sign it with a permanent marker (white works best on slate or stone), and place it in a bucket. One side can be for the guest's name, while the other can be for a word of advice or well wishes for the bride and groom.

By its natures, a tree slice is a blank canvas that becomes a work of art with the signatures of your guests. A permanent marker works best, especially one with a fine or medium tip.

A wooden bench is an unconventional guest-book idea, but it makes perfect sense if you plan to install the bench in your home or on your porch. Ask guests to sign the slats of wood across the back or along the arm rests, and spray it with a clear coat after the wedding (especially if the bench will be used outdoors).

Buy two wooden monograms of your initials and us it as a guest-book alternative. Display it in your home after the wedding. Pine wood letters are another option, which can be propped on your mantel or bookshelf later.

A "tree" thumbprint guest book is a popular idea that also works as home decor. A large print of a tree with naked branches is placed onto a table, with ink pads and pens nearby. The guest steps up to the table, places his or her thumb onto an ink pad, and presses the thumbprint onto an area of the tree to create a "leaf." The thumbprint dries quickly, allowing the guest to then sign his or her name over it. Frame the print after the wedding and enjoy!

## favors

Gift your guests handcrafted goodies like miniature homemade pies placed in boxes, homemade cookies in glassine envelopes, or local saltwater taffy in stamped kraft-paper bags. Macaroon favors placed in boxes also make a terrific (and tasty) take-home favors. Small jars of local goods — like honey, jam, or syrup — are also crowd-pleasers which can be embellished with a custom wedding label and decorative striped

twine. A simple kraft-paper sticker can customize any wedding favor, from a jar of jam to a bar of homemade soap.

Go green with organic wedding favors, like potted plants or herbs. Place the plants on a table where guests can grab one on the way home. I like this idea because it is a gift you know they'll enjoy — and it won't be a favor that gets tossed away.

When selecting your rustic favors, consider the time of year you'll be tying the knot. If your wedding is in the fall, gift miniature pumpkin pies, cranberry jam, or small glass bottles of apple cider. If you're planning a summer wedding, think about the quintessential summertime treat — s'mores! Assemble two graham crackers, a marshmallow, and a chocolate bar in a clear bag, closed tightly with twine. Include instructions for making the s'more.

I'm a coffee fanatic, so the idea of receiving local coffee beans as a favor sounds great. If you, too, love coffee, you can purchase local coffee beans and place them in a small drawstring burlap bag, with a tag that provides information on the origin of the beans and the flavor.

For a surefire wedding favor, set up a candy "buffet." A candy buffet (or bar) is a table that includes large, apothecary glass jars filled with taffy, chocolate, caramel, lollipops, and more. Guests can step up to the table and fill a bag with sweets to go. I recommend that you select candies that tie into your color palette (you can shop at Candy Warehouse by color), and allot about half a pound of candy per guest to ensure that the jars are full, not sparse. Pair the jars with candy scoops, which can be found online. Clearly label each jar with a handwritten tag or card.

## the cake

How you display your cake is just as important as the cake itself. For this theme, a cake looks best when set atop a wooden pedestal, birch-bark slab, galvanized-metal pedestal, or square wooden platform. Whether you plan to serve one cake or five varieties of cakes and pies, each dessert deserves to be put on a pedestal!

Any wedding cake can be transformed with the help of a custom cake topper, a stand, or a handcrafted accent. For instance, a traditional three-tiered cake becomes rustic chic in an instant with succulents and a wooden cake stand.

Another down-home approach is to wrap grapevine around the bottom of the cake stand. A simple chalkboard cake topper — which you can find at a craft store or Gartner Studios — can be personalized with your own message. Add "Happily Ever After," "Just Married," or your initials.

When shopping for my own cake topper, I had a difficult time finding a set that looked like us. If you're searching for a custom topper that resembles you as a couple — capturing your unique look, with a birdcage veil for you and a beard for him, for instance — consider ordering a personalized set, like this charming example by Wood & Grain, below right.

Another idea is a pair of woodland animals — like deer, for instance — set atop the cake. You can find small animal figurines at craft stores, toy stores, and even most dollar stores. You can also find figurines that reflect your love of gardening, kayaking, or hiking.

Or, think about shaping toppers from marzipan or fondant (or have someone do it for you).

Adorn your cake using natural materials, such a twig cake topper. This type of topper is fashioned to form a couple's monogram or to spell out "I Do."

A do-it-yourself topper that's just as adorable as it is inexpensive is one made from birch bark and a wooden dowel. Cut a heart shape from a sheet of birch bark with sharp scissors; attach the back of the heart to a wooden dowel, using a dab of hot glue. Allow it to dry overnight; then place the dowel directly into the top of your cake.

Also be on the lookout for rustic-chic cake toppers like a pair of love birds made of linen or clay; a Western-themed bride and groom with cowboy hats and boots; a "just married" cake banner made from linen bunting, string, and twigs. I've even seen pine cone cake toppers, donning a top hat and veil, which proves that with a little creativity, you can turn nearly any object into a beloved cake topper.

If you're serving cupcakes, set up a homespun display by placing them on a birch tree slice or birch cake stand (available from Roxy Heart Vintage).

As an alternative to a traditional wedding cake, offer a dessert bar with home-baked pies, cookies, or cupcakes. Or, provide a soft-serve ice-cream machine, or even a do-it-yourself ice-cream-sundae bar. Incorporate details such as birch cupcake stands, a decorative table garland (it can read something like "Love Is Sweet"), and cupcake toppers.

# Resources

Page 57

Amanda Day Rose / www.amandadayrose.com;

Wood & Grain / www.etsy.com/shop/woodandgrain;

Avery / www.avery.com;

Etsy / www.etsy.com;

Emmaline Bride / www.emmalinebride.com

Page 58

Amanda Day Rose / www.amandadayrose.com

Page 59

Amanda Day Rose / www.amandadayrose.com;

Page 60

Wood & Grain / www.ctsy.com/shop/woodandgrain;

Jen Simpson Design / www.jensimpsondesign.com

Page 62

National Park Service / www.nps.gov

Page 66

Etsy / www.etsy.com;

Roxy Heart Vintage / www.etsy.com/shop/RoxyHeartVintage

Page 69

Chiavari / www.chiavarichairs.com

Page 71

PNZ Designs / www.PNZDesigns.com

Page 72

Little Hunny Studio / www.etsy.com/shop/LittleHunnyStudio

Page 75

New Bride Co. / www.etsy.com/shop/NewBrideCo

Kristin Coffin Jewelry / www.KristinCoffin.com

Page 88

Luna Bazaar / www.lunabazaar.com

Page 95

Candy Warehouse / www.CandyWarehouse.com

Page 96

Gartner Studios / www.gartnerstudios.com

Wood & Grain / www.ctsy.com/shop/woodandgrain;

Page 98

Roxy Heart Vintage / www.RoxyHeartVintage.com

# Beach Bliss

Sand, sunshine, and gently rolling waves . . .
what's not to love about the beach? It's no
surprise that a beach-themed wedding has
become a popular choice for couples, as it
provides a gorgeous backdrop, warm weather,
and beautiful light, plus relaxation and
tranquility for you and your guests.

# Invitations & More

The first impression that your guests will have of your upcoming wedding is the engagement photograph — if you decide to do it. Not every couple schedules a session with their wedding photographer, and I don't understand why! The engagement photo session is a great way to get to know your photographer — plus it's the perfect opportunity to creatively work your theme into the shot and give your guests a hint of what the wedding day will bring. And, could there be a more fun way to introduce yourselves as a couple than to use the photo on your save the date?

## save-the-date cards

Once the wedding date is set, the venue is booked, and the engagement photo is ready, it's time to formally announce to guests: "We're getting married!" If you're considering carrying a beach theme all the way through your big day, from inception to reception, the perfect place to begin is with your save the date.

A save the date graciously gives guests advance notice for travel arrangements. It can be as simple or as detailed as you'd like, provided it will not upstage your invitations.

Karen & John

SAVE THE DATE

Karen & John

AUGUST THIRD
TWO THOUSAND TWELVE

MAUI

invitation to follow
WWW.RITTERTOBE.COM

A beach wedding's color palette typically includes the color blue, inspired by both sea and sky, along with natural colors, such as a shade of green, beige, or even bronze. If you've made a decision on a nautical wedding, and your ceremony and reception are at a marina, for example, a palette of navy blue and white — plus an added accent color — sets the tone perfectly. Some interesting accent colors are red, green, orange, or yellow. Navy blue and white,

being the primary colors, can carry throughout most of your decor — invitations, centerpieces, and table linens, for instance — while the accent color should pop in unexpected places (like red shoes for the bride or a yellow bow tie for the groom).

Creating your own save-the-date cards can be a special project you both will enjoy. Use your color palette, choose a motif or two (an anchor, sailboat, or starfish, for example), and create a simple design "frame." You can upload your design and photo to an online service and have it print the cards for you, or you can do your own printing at home.

If you don't have time to create the save the dates yourself — and you'd prefer an expert's design — consider a beach- and travel-inspired save-the-date luggage tag from Mavora Art and Design (on page 103), ideal for destination weddings.

Or this save the date, from Starboard Press on the opposite page, a fun and whimsical announcement, it exudes a beachy feel with rolling blue waves and sunny skies. It is informative and tells guests the basics: who is getting married, and when and where

the wedding will be held. This is a perfect example of a save the date to select when you are planning a beach wedding without a specific color palette picked out just yet.

Do you want to recite your vows on the beach? Give guests the heads-up with a save the date featuring flip-flop sandals or a photo of your names written in the sand. Is a ceremony at a marina in order? I love this card from Wide Eyes Design, left. It incorporates the couple's nautical palette of blue, white, and gold, with striping along the sides.

Whether you create your own design or work with a designer, your save-the-date cards can be so much fun. What a great way to express yourselves and announce that you two will unite in marriage. Next up, the invitations!

## invitations

The wedding invitation does not necessarily have to coordinate with the save the date, but it should impart a similar tone. Beach weddings and nautical weddings tend to be less formal, so your invitation can follow suit.

The best wedding invitations, in my opinion, successfully do two things: convey the theme and enthuse the recipient. Your wedding will be the party of the year; as such, it deserves the type of announcement that builds anticipation.

If I received this fun, passport-style wedding invitation (by Serendipity Beyond Design, right), I would be ready to pack my bags! Perfect for a destination wedding, a complete "package" like this can contain a passport photo of you and your spouse-to-be, a boarding pass, and a passport-style booklet complete with an itinerary and accommodation suggestions. Likewise, an invitation with a beach-inspired motif gives your guests a glimpse into the sandy-shore ceremony that awaits.

When you discover an accent that inspires you — like the playful nautical "love" knot (from {via}vacious Designs above right), or the anchor above left, from Amanda Day Rose — use it throughout your entire decor plan. You'll have a cohesively themed wedding, and it will continue to inspire you throughout the planning process. The detail that inspires you the most deserves to be the focal point of your fête.

Once you select the perfect wedding invitation, don't forget to order the inclusions to accompany it. You will need reply cards, envelopes, a map with directions to the locale (optional), and, after the wedding, thank-you cards with envelopes. A reply card is smaller than the invitation and is accompanied by a matching envelope. It is what guests will use to let you know whether or not they will be in attendance. You should include your mailing address on the envelope, along with a postage stamp. For a cost-effective alternative, try a reply postcard instead, which is ideal for informal beach or nautical weddings. A reply postcard needs no envelope, and the rate for a postage stamp is less than a standard one (so you'll save some money along the way). Or bring the process completely into the 21st century by having guests send their RSVPs to your wedding Web site (be sure to include the e-mail address and URL of your site).

Each invitation will require an inner envelope and an outer envelope. The inner envelope is labeled with the guest's name, while the outer envelope includes his or her name and address, your return address, and postage.

Take a look at the wonderful graphics in a suite from Ruff House Art, opposite, and also the dramatic, striped envelope lining, below, from Amanda Day Rose

Finally, you may need to enclose a small map, showing the locations of the ceremony and the reception. You can use a mapping program online to create a custom map for your venue. Print it, and make copies at your local print shop (using card stock or a soft linen paper). Or order custom maps for your event; ask your stationer if he or she can customize a map to complement your invitation. This charming handmade map, right, is designed and hand lettered by Laura Hooper Calligraphy, as part of a beautiful, beach-inspired invitation suite.

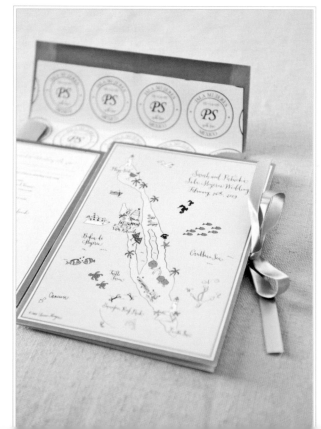

RESPOND BY NOVEMBER 23

NAMES _____

_____ attending   _____ not attending

_____ number of guests attending

together with their parents

JILL MORRISON

&

BRIAN SHEPHARD

invite you to share in the celebration of their marriage

saturday | december fourteenth | two thousand thirteen

six o'clock in the evening

first presbyterian church of fort lauderdale

401 se 13th avenue | fort lauderdale | florida

reception to follow

needhan estate | 828 se 4th street | fort lauderdale | florida

# The Ceremony

The wedding ceremony is one of the most memorable parts of the wedding day, brimming with joy, excitement, and anticipation. In this section, I'll discuss some ideas to take your beach (or nautical) wedding to the next level with a stunning location, aisle decorations, flower-girl baskets, handmade ring pillows, programs, and a section called Thoughtful Extras which includes suggestions your guests will really enjoy. First, let's pinpoint your perfect wedding location.

## where will you tie the knot?

Location, location, location! A beach wedding provides the perfect opportunity to celebrate in picturesque surroundings, with the waves at your back and the sand under your feet. Now is the time to scout settings nearby, or to search online for a destination location that suits your dream wedding. Look for resorts or beach clubs that offer complete wedding packages: a dedicated space and a professional team with the resources (microphone, speakers, seating, dance floor, bar and food service, and more) to make planning a cinch.

## decor

What's one major advantage of a beach wedding? The natural landscape is a beautiful, ready-made backdrop. Blue skies (or a sunset in the evening), gently rolling waves, and whispering sand contribute to a most romantic setting. All you have to do is set up seating and a ceremony space, and add a little personalization where you see fit.

If your ceremony will take place on the beach, use the surroundings to your advantage. For guest seating, you can rent plain white chairs or benches. Place the chairs or benches in rows with no decoration added, or with a simple flower or lengths of ribbon or fabric tied to the end of each row. Designate an aisleway with pebbles or seashells placed on either side. If you wish, have your flower girl sprinkle rose petals down the aisle, too. Kick off your shoes and walk barefoot (or wear sandals, in case the sand is very hot). Or, you could go for a traditional aisle runner.

While a beach wedding will look lovely as is, a few of your own embellishments can be added if you'd like. One of my favorite beach-ready decorations is a natural-raffia-and-starfish chair hanger from Beach Weddings by Bree, below.

Planning a sunset ceremony? Place battery-operated candles inside lanterns (you can find affordable lanterns at IKEA, or make your own with candles set in mason jars), and position them along the aisle for a romantic glow.

For a nautical wedding ceremony, be on the lookout for accents like a decorative oar, buoy, ship wheel, anchor, lighthouse, or sailboat, which can be found online at eBay or Etsy, or at craft stores. A clever accessory (and keepsake) is the nautical knot, which can be placed along the aisle, indoors or out.

FOCAL POINT

If you are reciting your vows on the beach, you may want to create a ceremonial focal point. An arch, altar, decorative backdrop, or chuppah are a few suggestions for your ceremony space. If you are getting married at a resort, check if it has these available for rent; you can also rent one from a local event/party company. If you're a daring do-it-yourselfer, you can make your own chic backdrop. Purchase supplies from Bamboo Expressions to build a bamboo arbor — just add side curtains. This ceremony site, above, was created for a unity ceremony.

## flower girl & ring bearer

Make sure the flower girl gets in on the beach-inspired fun with a basket or pail full of beach roses or seashells to toss down the aisle. Other options include carrying a ribbon wand, a parasol (which doubles as sun protection), or a pinwheel — or, if you have more than one flower girl, have each hold the end of a flower chain, garland, or wooden "Here Comes the Bride" sign.

For the ring bearer, consider nautical coordinates like an anchor-print pillow, or a navy-and-white-striped pillow with rope, like the one I spotted online at Lucky You Lucky Me, below right.

If a ring pillow isn't your style, seek an alternative, such as a large nautilus seashell, a sand-dollar "dish" with the rings placed inside, or a small, stamped muslin ring bag, personalized with a nautical motif or your initials and the wedding date.

## ceremony programs

If you'd like to offer programs to guests, you can print them yourself or have them custom made. Ask your invitation designer if he or she offers coordinating programs, which can be matched to your invitation for a cohesive look. If you plan on making your own accents, like programs or place cards, look for stamps at your craft store that feature anchors, starfish, or seashells. You'll have plenty of places to use them.

Ceremony programs can be placed in a basket near the entryway of your ceremony space or distributed by members of your wedding party before the nuptials begin. Look for ceremony programs that can double as fans; guests will value them if the weather is hot or humid!

If you'd rather skip the paper version, a ceremony program can be written on a framed chalkboard instead. On your "program," include the bride's and groom's names, wedding date, location, names of parents and attendants, lists of readings and songs, etc., and display the chalkboard on an easel near the entrance of your ceremony.

# thoughtful extras

If your wedding ceremony will take place outside, protect your guests from the sun, bugs, or a breezy day with a few simple comfort items that they will appreciate.

### WHICH WAY?

Before guests arrive at your beach ceremony, create and post a sign to direct them where to go, so they'll know they're on the right path (or boardwalk). You can make your own sign with wood, and white and black paint with a simple arrow

### WIND/COLD WEATHER

If your beach wedding will take place in cooler months — or if it happens to be cloudy, rainy, or windy — guests may get chilly. Provide a basket full of (again, inexpensive) shawls or blankets that will keep guests cozy. You can find fleece blankets at IKEA for around $2 each, or search your local dollar store, Target, or Walmart. You only need a few, not one per guest.

### SHOE BOX

Offer guests a convenient "shoe check" for their formal shoes. Create your own with wooden shelves and a simple sign that reads "Shoes Optional." You can also use white bins for guests to deposit their shoes; in a separate container, include pairs of flip-flops (buy them inexpensively, and in a range of sizes, at Old Navy or Target) for guests to wear on the sand.

## SUN

If you're lucky, your wedding day will feature sunshine and blue skies, without a drop of rain in sight. However, full sun means that guests will be squinting throughout the ceremony. Offer a basket or jar of inexpensive sunglasses (think dollar-store frames) for guests to grab on the way to their seats.

## BUGS

The most notorious wedding crashers at a beachside wedding are mosquitoes. You'll want to keep them at bay to ensure that guests are happily dancing and partying the night away — not swatting and reaching for bug-bite spray. If you're having the party at a private venue, have it fogged for mosquitoes the day before. And, just to be safe, keep bags of fabric-softener sheets nearby for guests to use — they actually repel those little pests.

## HEAT

It can get very hot and humid at a beach wedding. Give guests bottles of ice-cold water, which have been placed in coolers or ice buckets. You could offer paper fans or parasols, too, for guests to use to cool themselves. You can find personalized paper fans and parasols at Beau Coup or Luna Bazaar.

# The Attire

Now that you have a vision of the perfect ceremony location and accoutrements, it's time to decide what you'll wear on your big day. In this section, I'll inspire you with dress options, accessories, unique ways to cover up in case it's chilly, and ideas for what to wear in your hair.

## the bride

The beach wedding is synonymous with a low-key, casual atmosphere. The bride can follow suit with a casual, short dress or a long, flowy dress made from a lightweight, breathable material (like cotton or chiffon). Look for a neckline that flatters you best and suits your style, whether it is strapless, halter, sweetheart, one shoulder, or v-neck. Before you shop, get inspired by searching online (try Dessy, which allows you to narrow searches by neckline style, train length, dress length, and material) and by browsing wedding magazines. As a rule of thumb, always try on at least one dress style you may not have otherwise considered — it may end up being the most flattering on you!

After you've found the ideal dress, complement it with accessories that are simple, yet elegant. Add a pop of playful color to it with a flower belt or dress sash that borrows a shade from your color palette. For instance, if you are planning a nautical wedding and are using navy blue and white as your main colors, see how the bride incorporated her accent color in her earrings (below), in her ribbon sash (on pages 106 and 117), and in her bouquet wrap (on page 123). If you are getting married outdoors in the evening or in an off-season — when it might be cooler — consider a simple bridal bolero or shrug to wear with your dress.

Pair your dream wedding dress with a fitting hair accessory, such as this design, above, from Miss Ruby Sue. It features ivory fabric rosettes, feathers, and a hint of "something blue" — it's a beautiful alternative to a traditional bridal veil or a simple floral bloom. Or, consider a tulle bridal bow or a lace headband, depending on which flatters your hairstyle best. Some of my favorite beach-wedding hair accessories are starfish attached to bobby pins (find them at The Sunflower Stand). Or, go completely natural — beach weddings are made for no-fuss, hair-down styles.

If you plan to wear a veil, consider one with a comb that is attached lower on your head, so your veil won't blow around in your face. You could even opt for a birdcage veil, which is made with tulle netting designed to be worn close to your face. Another alternative is a blusher veil, which falls slightly above your shoulders.

As with your entire ensemble, your jewelry ought to stay natural and simple. A strand of pearls or a pair of drop earrings would be perfect beach-wedding wear.

If you can't decide between bare feet and flip-flops, or if you want something slightly dressier, consider a cross between the two! Barefoot sandals are a popular trend among beach brides and are akin to jewelry for your feet. The result is a dressed-up look and the illusion that you are wearing flip-flops, but your feet remain bare on the bottom. Try Beach Foot Jewelry as one resource.

## bridesmaids

When deciding on the perfect bridesmaid dress, remember, a shorter length is perfect. Select a color that complements your color palette, and choose a lightweight, comfortable, and breathable material. Casual and simple styles are best, so that your bridesmaids can wear their dresses again. Since the dress code is informal, you can select a shade and ask your bridesmaids to find a dress flattering in a particular neckline, you'll have a coordinated look, and they'll feel confident in their own hand-selected attire.

Jewelry is a popular item for the bride to give to her bridesmaids as a token of her appreciation. Select a piece of jewelry that borrows from your beach or nautical theme. For example, this charm bracelet, below right, with an anchor, starfish, and seashell charm, would be fitting for a beach wedding, while the nautical-knot bracelet and the silver-anchor pendant necklace, below center and left, both from Junghwa by Amy Stewart, are sweet and memorable, and are perfect for either bridesmaids or a flower girl.

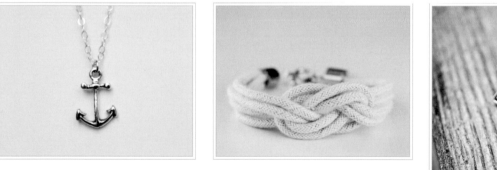

### FLOWER GIRL & RING BEARER

The flower girl is happiest when she's comfortable. Ensure her joy for the day with a pretty, lightweight dress in a natural fabric, like organic cotton. You can find eco-friendly, organic-cotton flower-girl dresses at Olive & Fern that have been flower-girl tested — and approved. A pillowcase-style dress, which is rectangular in shape and cinches at the top with fabric or a ribbon, is another airy option that is casual enough for a beach ceremony.

As with the flower girl, the ring bearer should be comfortable in what he wears on the beach. A seersucker (or soft cotton) suit is one example, paired with a button-down shirt, suspenders, dress pants, and maybe a bow tie. A tie is optional, but if worn, it should coordinate with the groomsmen's ties. Shoes — perhaps sandals — should be comfortable enough to walk in the sand.

## the groom & groomsmen

The groom should coordinate with the bride and bridesmaids in a laid-back, low-key, coastal fashion. For beach-casual style, a light-colored suit (like white or khaki) is best, paired with a tie. For a nautical wedding, incorporate anchors or a navy-and-white chevron pattern on the groom's bow tie. For an even less formal look, skip the tie and opt for a white linen button-down shirt and linen pants, paired with deck shoes, sandals, or bare feet.

# The Flowers

For a beach-wedding bouquet, hydrangeas, anemones, calla lilies, dahlias, gerbera daisies, palm fronds, wild grasses, and beach roses are just a few suggestions that come to mind. When browsing bouquets, be on the lookout for bright, eccentric hues and natural options, too — like wheat, tied with a simple lace ribbon.

Bring the beach to your bouquet with capiz shells, which you can find at Shell Outlet, or wrap your bouquet hand with a navy-and-white-striped grosgrain ribbon (see Ribbon and Bows Oh My!) for a nautical touch.

To honor a loved one who has passed, a small locket with a photo enclosed can be pinned to your bouquet handle. Lockets with photo enclosures can be found at your local craft or jewelry shop.

For a beach wedding, look for bouquets that incorporate natural elements, like seashells, sand dollars, and starfish. One such example is a handmade bouquet that combines seashells, blue gems, and foam-like flowers, like this creation, left, by The Bridal Flower.

Thinking of ditching a traditional bouquet in lieu of an alternative? Carry a palm-leaf raffia fan from Oriental Trading, a pinwheel from Pinwhirls, a paper-flower bouquet from The Little Red Button, peacock feathers, or a parasol down the aisle — and have your bridesmaids follow suit.

The groom, groomsmen, father of the bride, father of the groom, and ring bearer should all have a boutonniere. Traditionally, floral boutonnieres are the norm, but they tend to wilt quickly in the sun and will only last for one day. Instead, opt for an alternative that will last forever. A sand dollar, starfish, or seashell can be made into a surprisingly effortless boutonniere with a dab of hot glue and a pin back (found at Michaels or Jo-Ann stores). Or, browse handmade options, like this simple yet stunning sea-urchin boutonniere from Fairyfolk Weddings, below right, perfectly fitting for a seaside wedding. Below left and center are two unconventional boutonnieres from designer Amber Steffe of The Sunflower Stand.

The boutonniere usually coordinates with the bouquets carried by the bride and her bridesmaids. For instance, if the bridesmaids are carrying simple wheat bouquets, the boutonniere should follow suit, but in a smaller size.

# The Reception

Let the fun begin! Greet your guests with three key items as they enter your reception space: a refreshing beverage, an escort card that indicates the table where they will be sitting, and plenty of decorative, themed elements to let them know that it's time to relax and enjoy the festivities. You'll also need flowers, some fun activities for adults and children, cake, and wedding favors; I've got loads of ideas in this section. First, let's focus on the location of your reception: where will the party take place?

## the venue

A beach or nautical wedding reception centers around one important element: water. Whether your reception is held on the beach, near the beach, in a restaurant overlooking a marina, or in a cottage near a lake, water should be the focal point of your event.

If you plan to have your reception take place immediately following your ceremony, consider a tented reception on or near your selected beach location. A tented reception gives guests the freedom to be outside, while still having a covered space for dinner (or inclement weather).

A wonderful idea for a beach wedding is to have the ceremony on the beach, followed by the reception at a beach house nearby. One of my favorite vacation spots is North Carolina, particularly the Outer Banks. There, you can find plenty of houses for rent during the summer months — many with enough rooms to accomodate your entire wedding party! Plus, these homes are accessible to the beach and within foot travel to the ceremony. You can have on-site catering, a cocktail hour, and dancing all outdoors, with a sunset at night and the sound of crashing waves.

If your reception will include a tent, take it from boring to beautiful with handcrafted details: add your own fabric bunting (made with fabric remnants from a craft store and twine), plus white party lights, lanterns, or battery-operated lights in mason jars to add a romantic glow.

## escort cards

As your guests enter your reception space, wow them with the environment you've created. Your escort cards — which inform guests of their table assignments — should be front and center and easily seen by them upon their arrival. Escort cards are another part of the wedding celebration where you can have great fun. Folded tent cards (available at Staples or OfficeMax), are the simplest, just print from your computer or handwrite. Arrange them on a tray of seashells or smooth rocks on a table near the entrance.

If you're limited on space — or prefer to nix the cards altogether — opt for a large seating chart that can be placed on an easel instead. Browse designs online at The Seating Chart Boutique.

One of my favorite ideas for escort cards incorporates a nautical-inspired favor. The brilliant creations by Laura Hooper Calligraphy, above right and below left, combine the guests name and table number with a keepsake sea urchin or a compass — what a charming reminder of your wedding!

Similarly, a sand dollar with a handwritten table assignment makes an equally memorable solution and takes care of two wedding must-haves (an escort card and a favor).

## cocktail hour

For a beach wedding, the appetizer menu practically writes itself; offer a selection of seafood specialties like shrimp cocktail or crab cakes for guests to enjoy while sipping mojitos, sangria, or piña coladas. For a casual bar, use mason jars as drinking glasses, and complete the look with striped

straws (try Cute Tape)in hues borrowed from your color palette. Or, instead of mason-jar glasses, serve up cocktails in coconut party cups — which can be found at local party-supply stores — to evoke a luau-paradise vibe.

Arrange your drinking glasses near a beverage bar, where glass drink dispensers (the style with a spigot) have been filled with iced tea, lemonade, or punch. Add a label to clearly identify each drink. If you're planning a tented reception and have little room, buy stackable drink dispensers (available on Amazon), so you can offer more beverages without sacrificing valuable table space.

## guest book

Invite guests to leave their well wishes and signatures, using a unique guest-book alternative. For example, offer a basket of seashells and fine-point permanent markers. Place the shells and markers on a table, along with an extra basket labeled for signed shells. Each guest can select a shell, sign his or her name, and place it in the signed-shell basket. After the wedding, place the shells in a large jar — like an apothecary jar, for instance — and display it in your home as a wedding-day keepsake. (You can also use large river stones, sea glass, or sand dollars instead of shells.)

A larger object that ties into a beach or nautical theme — like a ukulele, ship wheel, wooden anchor (try Nautical Seasons), faux buoy, or paddle oar — can be signed with a simple permanent marker. If the object is metal or dark, use a metallic permanent marker so that signatures will show.

Or, place a photo matt over one of your favorite beach-inspired engagement photos. Invite guests to sign directly on the matt, and have the photo framed after the wedding to display in your home.

## tables & centerpieces

Design your table settings and centerpieces with a natural, low key, and relaxed mood in mind. Consider floral centerpieces, which are incredibly versatile and can coordinate with nearly any color palette. Placing white hydrangeas in mason jars or glass vases is one such example.

A favorite do-it-yourself and surprisingly chic centerpiece uses test-tube vials (yes, the kind you used in chemistry class) filled with ranunculus and baby's breath, and placed in sleek wooden vase holders. You can find test-tube vases online, and wooden vase holders can also be found online at Heirloom Woodwork.

If you plan to use long, formal dining tables, an elegant table runner provides a dramatic pop of color atop a white tablecloth. For centerpieces, use simple glass vases to hold white pillar candles — my favorite nonfloral alternative.

If your dining tables are elegant as is, show off their innate beauty and add a simple, natural touch: set different-size jars on birch-tree slices and place them along a table runner (see photo on opposite page). Birch-tree slices can be found in a variety of sizes online from the Birch Bark Store.

Find inventive ways to use color in your table decor. Fill glass vases of different sizes with simple white and pale-colored flowers and greenery, to enhance a white tablecloth with an accent shade. Turquoise blue (in the photograph above) looks very "beachy" atop a white tablecloth and is especially fitting for a seaside theme.

You can also introduce color in your chair covers or table napkins, which look lovely when paired against a standard white tablecloth.

## reception decor

Throughout your reception area, incorporate details from your theme: display ship wheels, anchors, or miniature life preservers, or decorate a tiered cedar wood piling (a wooden post that resembles a pier piling) with candles. Cedar pilings can be found online at Nautical Seasons.

Create a nautical vignette onshore with a canoe, life raft, and rope. Arrange wood pallets into a makeshift "dock," tie the canoe to wood stumps to look as though it's "docked," and line the walkway with white lanterns.

Be sure to include decorations in unexpected places, such as on a side table or near your cake. One such example is different types of knotted-rope, placed on a wooden board and framed (see photo on opposite page).

After your cocktail hour — and the bride and groom's main entrance — it's time for guests to eat. At a beach wedding, a buffet can be more practical and less formal than a traditional sit-down dinner. Decorate your buffet table with colorful napkins in shades borrowed from your palette; place utensils in decorative baskets or pails wrapped in rope or twine.

## activities for kids & adults

Keep kids (and adults) at your reception occupied with some fun activities. One of my favorite ideas is to learn how to tie a few different nautical knots. Print step-by-step instructions and provide lengths of rope for the kids. Place all of the supplies at a separate table, along with chairs, so that kids can sit and give it a try.

Another option is to set up a coloring station for kids, with boxes of crayons and nautical-themed coloring pages (which can be printed from the online shop The Coloring Spot).

Adults need fun activities, too! Dancing is, of course, always a popular pastime at receptions. Offer additional activities to increase the fun factor, like horseshoes on the beach or a corn toss, both of which guests can play during the cocktail hour or after dinner.

One of my favorite reception activities is a photo booth, which can also be used to enhance your guest book. To make your own photo booth, you'll need to create a backdrop, using patterned fabric, paper, or a simple fabric garland hung across a back wall. Nearby, place a Polaroid camera (and plenty of film) on a table, with instructions for guests to snap a photo and paste it into your guest book. Include pens so guests can sign under the photos and add well wishes for you.

## cake

How will you decorate your cake? It's all in the topper! Consider a pair of wooden miniature Adirondack chairs, personalized with your initials or "Mr." and "Mrs.," from Rustic Blend; a limpet-shell monogram topper from the online store By the Seashore; or amazing chocolate seashell candies that look almost too real to eat from Andie's Specialty Sweets.

You can embellish the simplest cake with charming beach accents. Transform a traditional white buttercream wedding cake with faux starfish or sand dollars cascading along the tiers. Sugary fondant anchors or sea horses are other beach-themed decorating options.

## wedding favors

The best wedding favors are either one of two things: a) functional, or b) edible. I've found plenty of both that your guests will love. Sea-glass candy is one favorite, because it incorporates a beach element with an edible favor, and it can be sweetly packaged in a muslin favor bag and gifted to guests. Muslin favor bags, right, can be hand stamped with an anchor, seashell, starfish, or compass, plus your initials and your wedding date.

You can create a nautical or beach-inspired candy buffet with various sizes of jars from Amazon, or find glass containers at thrift stores or craft stores), wrap ribbon, and apply paper labels printed right from your computer. Buy silver-colored candy scoops at Candy Warehouse and plenty of candy for placing in the jars.

Seashell tealight candles are a welcome beach-themed favor, and they provide guests with a special memory of your beach wedding. They can be found online at Beach Weddings by Bree.

Shell-shaped soaps from Soap Cafe or anchor-shaped soaps found at Latika Soap are popular among guests, because everyone can use soap! Plus, it's one favor that is used until it's gone, so you know that your gift will be appreciated.

Other examples of wedding favors to tie into your beach or nautical theme include wine-bottle buoy charms, anchor-themed drink coasters, hand-painted sailboat or lighthouse ornaments, or nautical-knot wine-bottle toppers.

## after dinner

After dinner, cake, and coffee have been served, offer guests a few different activities to wind down the evening.

Invite a cigar roller to hand roll cigars and offer them to guests. Be sure to have personalized matchbooks available. Have a bonfire at dusk, complete with s'mores, hanging lanterns, and comfortable chairs. Provide plenty of firewood and inexpensive fleece throws to keep guests to keep comfortable and don't forget the sparkler send-off at the end of the evening.

# Resources

Page 104
Mavora Art and Design / www.mavora.com;
Starboard Press / www.etsy.com/shop/starboardpress;
Wide Eyes Design / wideeyesdesign.com

Page 105
Serendipity Beyond Design

Page 107
{via}vacious Design / www.etsy.com/shop/viavaciousdesigns;
Amanda Day Rose / www.etsy.com/shop/AmandaDayRose;

Page 108
Ruff House Art / www.ruffhouseart.com;
Amanda Day Rose / www.etsy.com/shop/AmandaDayRose;
Laura Hooper Calligraphy / www.etsy.com/shop/LHCalligraphy

Page 111
Beach Weddings by Bree / www.etsy.com/shop/
beachweddingsbybree;

Page 112
Bamboo Expressions / www.bambooexpressions.com

Page 113
Lucky You Lucky Me / www.etsy.com/shop/
LuckyYouLuckyMe

Page 116
Beau Coup / www.beau-coup.com/paper-parasols;
Luna Bazaar / www.lunabazaar.com/paper-parasols;
Dessy / www.dessy.com

Page 118
Miss Ruby Sue / www.etsy.com/shop/missrubysue;
Beach Foot Jewelry / www.beachfootjewelry.com;
The Sunflower Stand / www.etsy.com/shop/thesunflowerstand

Page 119
Junghwa by Amy Stewart / www.etsy.com/shop/junghwa

Page 121
Olive & Fern / www.etsy.com/shop/OliveandFern

Page 123
Shell Outlet / www.shelloutlet.com;
Ribbon and Bows Oh My! / www.ribbonandbowsohmy.com;

The Bridal Flower / www.thebridalflower.com

Page 125
Oriental Trading / www.orientaltrading.com;
Pinwhirls / www.pinwhirls.com;
The Little Red Button / www.thelittleredbutton.com;
Fairyfolk Weddings, www.etsy.com/shop/fairyfolkweddings;
The Sunflower Stand / www.etsy.com/shop/thesunflowerstand

Page 127
The Seating Chart Boutique / www.seatingchartboutique;
Laura Hooper Calligraphy / www.etsy.com/shop/LHCalligraphy

Page 128
Cute Tape / www.cutetape.com

Page 129
Nautical Seasons / www.nauticalseasons.com

Page 130
Heirloom Woodwork / www.heirloomwoodwork.com;
Birch Bark Store / www.birchbarkstore.com

Page 132
Nautical Seasons / www.nauticalseasons.com

Page 133
The Coloring Spot / www.thecoloringspot.com

Page 135
Rustic Blend / www.rusticblend.com;
By the Seashore Decor / www.etsy.com/shop/
ByTheSeashoreDecor;
Andie's Specialty Sweets / www.etsy.com/shop/
andiespecialtysweets;
Candy Warehouse / www.candywarehouse.com

Page 136
Beach Weddings by Bree / www.etsy.com/shop/
beachweddingsbybree;
Soap Cafe / www.soapcafe.com;
Latika Soap / www.latikasoap.com

# Urban Chic

Do you love the big city? Do you dream of getting married in an upscale restaurant, downtown on a rooftop, or inside an art gallery? Are you drawn to bold, attention-grabbing prints, patterns, and typography? If so, a urban wedding may be the perfect choice for you. In this chapter, I'll show you how to plan a chic, stylish wedding from start to finish. I'll share ideas on what to wear, where to tie the knot, favors for guests, and more.

# Invitations & More

Urban-chic weddings often demonstrate a restrained approach, but that doesn't mean that bold graphics, elaborate designs, and a color palette that features metallic ink are out of the running when it comes to your printed materials. A good place to begin to explore this theme, and how much fun it can be, is with the invitations.

## invitation suites

One of the great things about the process of choosing your wedding invitations is that it happens months before your big day. Everyone knows that planning a wedding can be a little stressful, but in the beginning, the choice of vendors, the guest list, and the celebration plans are all distant thoughts. Now is the fun part, so enjoy it!

Using a variety of font sizes, neon colors, and a trendy layout, this suite from Daydream Prints, above left, combines these playful elements into a cohesive and strikingly modern look that can be employed on everything from your paper needs to your reception decor.

Planning a wedding in a big city? Let the city's skyline or other distinctive features be your motif and inspire your invitations. This urban-chic invitation by Serendipity Beyond Design, above right, is inspired by the subway-system signage and skyline of Miami, Florida.

Do you dream of traveling to exotic, faraway lands? Jen Simpson Design has created a beautifully composed suite inspired by such dreams, opposite.

For a modern wedding, an itinerary adds a fun and personalized touch you won't find in other themes. It can be designed to give your wedding party an idea of where to be and when to get there, or to provide guests with background information on the details of the day.

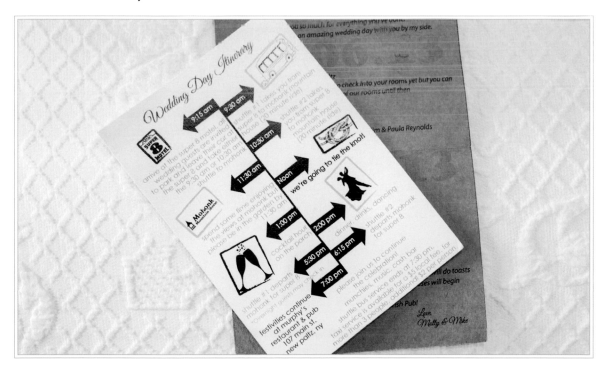

Planning a night under the stars? Consider a downtown soiree and a wedding invitation to match, like this beautiful, cosmic-themed suite designed by Hoopla Love, below. The watercolor effect, paired with the ethereal handwriting, makes an eye-catching collection.

# The Ceremony

The ceremony is the most important part of your wedding. It's where you'll exchange vows and declare your love for each other, while the people you love witness one of the most memorable days of your life. Picking the perfect ceremony site, then, is essential. In this section, I'll share some of my favorite types of urban-chic venues.

## the venue

When you're browsing for a modern wedding location, consider all of the possibilities. For instance, in places like Chicago, Seattle, and Los Angeles, there are grand hotels, with even grander ballrooms — but these venues are not just limited to big cities. Many hotels can literally provide everything you need, from guest accomodations to on-site catering and dance bands. Some restaurants, especially in larger cities, offer private rooms or outdoor event space. Museums, art galleries, rooftop lofts, waterfront sites, and even Central Park in New York City are all potential wedding venues. If you're looking for something a bit more adventurous, consider the wealth of converted warehouses and former factories that are now extravagant party spaces. Urban chic is everywhere!

I attended a wedding in Chicago where the outside of the building looked like a warehouse, yet the inside was completely renovated, with hardwood floors, exposed brick, and bare rafters. The guests enjoyed an elegant cocktail party, followed by dinner, drinks, and dancing. With its modern, industrial decor, it was unlike any other wedding I have attended.

Worried that the industrial-chic look won't be romantic enough for your ceremony? Add instant softness by decorating an arch or chuppah with white tulle.

If you're a bride who loves all eyes (and lights) on you, consider a theater stage, complete with professional lighting, your names and the wedding date projected onto a wall or a big screen, and bright white chairs for guests. This type of venue mimics the look and feel of a media event — and if you didn't already feel like the star of the show, you certainly will here.

A museum or modern-art gallery is a favorite choice for the couple looking to tie the knot in contemporary surroundings. If the weather permits, have the ceremony outdoors, where everyone can admire the skyline. Afterward, move the party inside for the cocktail hour, where guests can sip, mingle, and admire the artwork on display. Look for a gallery space that boasts white walls, lots of bright lighting, and enough room for dancing, once the tables are moved.

If your wedding will be outside, be prepared for inclement weather. Find out whether the venue has a tent or awning available for events or if they can suggest a rental company. You also may be responsible for renting tables and chairs. Other considerations include: Will you have to bring in a caterer? Is there a kitchen? How about parking?

## traditions

You may have heard of a unity ceremony, but what does it really mean? This ceremony uses a candle to symbolize the unity of two people becoming one (as two flames come together to make a single light). However, unity can be expressed in a variety of meaningful ways. A more modern variation is the wine ceremony. You'll need two carafes that have each been filled with a small amount of wine (choose two different types of wine, such as a white and a red), plus one empty glass. Each of you will take a carafe and pour your wine, in unison, into the empty glass. Then you'll each drink from the communal glass, as a symbol of your unity. (I recommend using very mild varieties of wine, so that they are palatable and mix well together.) Look online at Etsy for Scissor Mill, they make personalized carafes and glasses.

Another way to confirm your union is with a sand ceremony. Purchase two colors of sand and three clear, glass containers. Before the wedding, one color of sand is poured into container one, and the other color is poured into container two. Then, during the ceremony, both of you will pour the sand simultaneously into container three, so that it mixes completely. The mixture of the sand represents the combining of your lives.

## seating

In a traditional wedding ceremony, guests sit on a particular side, depending on whether they're part of the bride's or the groom's family. But some modern couples are approaching seating from a more contemporary angle: pick a seat, not a side. This arrangement encourages guests to socialize and get to know each other.

If you're having a rooftop wedding, a ballroom wedding, or a wedding in another unconventional venue, you may be renting chairs for guests. One of my favorite (and thoroughly modern) chair ideas is the "ghost chair."

A ghost chair is made entirely from clear polycarbonate (see p. 165, top center, for a table set with these chairs). The chair looks nearly invisible, which means that more emphasis is placed on the natural scenery or the decor. Try Chiavari, which offers a clear acrylic version of the company's most notable design.

A unique chair is one way to differentiate your wedding; how you arrange the chairs is another. Ceremony chairs are traditionally positioned in aisles and rows, but a contemporary wedding is the perfect occasion for changing the rules. Chairs can be placed in a circle, with an aisle for walking in one area and a central location for exchanging vows. This configuration gives every guest a close-up view of the wedding couple. In lieu of a circle, you could arrange chairs in a swirling pattern, which creates a long aisle where you can see everyone along the way.

## aisle decor

An urban-chic wedding is all about tweaking classic wedding customs to make them more contemporary. For example, a petal-strewn aisle is traditional; using ombre petals is a fresh approach. To achieve this look, sprinkle petals just along the edges of your aisle. Use petals in shades of deep red, hot pink, and white, for example. The petals should be strewn from darker to lighter: at the entrance of the aisle, distribute the deep-red petals, then introduce the hot-pink petals, and gradually blend in the white petals near the focal point, altar, or chuppah. Check Sparkle Soiree online for silk petals in an array of colors.

Petals can also be arranged into patterns, such as circles, or they can be used to form a custom monogram.

If your reception offers beautiful flooring, skip the aisle runner and show off the wood grain; instead of tossing petals, sprinkle gold or silver sequins or glitter (if your venue allows it). Keep in mind, though, that you'll probably end up with sequins or glitter on your gown. If you're concerned about this issue, consider using white feathers instead. They look stunning when strewn along an aisle, and since they're white, they won't impact the bride's gown.

Decorate chairs with low-profile embellishments, like an arrangement of greenery in a glass vase. Pick a small vase with a hook for hanging, attach a ribbon, and hang it from a chair back.

Or, for an understated, chic, and sophisticated effect, line the aisle with tall glass vases filled with long calla lilies.

## ring bearer & flower girl

Want your ring bearer to carry a more modern item than a pillow? Have him deliver the rings in a ring dish, or in a cube-shaped or hexagonal box. LV Woodworks on Etsy has a beautifully designed small wooden box. Or, tie the rings to a small origami crane, using a sturdy piece of thread strung through the paper. The ring bearer could also carry a memento instead — such as a zinc frame with a photo of the wedding couple — which he can place on a table at the focal point of your ceremony.

Love the idea of a ring "pillow," but want an updated look? Find a pillow in an ombre pattern or a punchy print, like plaid, houndstooth, or polka dots. Fun patterns, textures, and unexpected color combinations like neon yellow and ivory will keep your wedding fresh, current, and chic.

Who says your handsome pup can't do the job? Embellish his collar with a geometric bow (like this one from Little Blue Feathers, above) to reinforce your theme.

The flower girl traditionally tosses petals. But for a modern wedding, try one of these variations: have her carry your train down the aisle, give her a bouquet of colorful round balloons, or ask her to toss paper confetti instead of flower petals. Check out Flower Fetti online at Etsy for some great confetti ideas. You could also make her a ribbon wand by tying bright ribbons to a wooden dowel. Or, create a sequined flower-girl wand: attach a large wooden star or heart (found at a craft store) to a wooden dowel, using hot glue or wood glue. Adorn the star or heart with sequins, applying them with hot glue.

Finish the wand with a silver or gold ribbon (depending on the color of the sequins), tying it in a bow under the star or heart.

For a modern twist, have more than one ring bearer or flower girl, and give them something to carry down the aisle together, like a floral garland or a whimsical wedding banner.

## ceremony programs

A ceremony program can inform guests about your ceremony, as well as introduce the members of your wedding party. A ceremony program is optional; however, it does help guests by showing how the ceremony will unfold.

You may think that a ceremony program has to be formal, but it can actually be quite simple. I once saw a booklet-style wedding program, which the couple had made on their home printer. The program gave guests all sorts of information on the wedding, from why there was a certain theme to what time the reception would begin. It even listed local places to visit before the reception, just in case the guests had time to fill.

Instead of a traditional booklet or a single sheet of card stock, consider a contemporary alternative: turn your program into a fan, by attaching a piece of wood to make a handle. Opt for a design that reflects your overall theme, such as this watercolor creation from Hoopla Love, right.

## wedding-party gifts

A thoughtful, personalized gift for members of your wedding party is a perfect way to say "thanks." A token of your appreciation for all their hard work and dedication will mean a lot.

Inviting prospective bridesmaids to be members of your wedding party is one of the most exciting things to do after getting engaged.

A clutch purse is a traditional bridesmaid gift that can be easily adapted to your modern, urban-chic theme. Instead of choosing a conventional style, select a clutch in a fun, graphic material, such as a chevron pattern, stripes, or polka dots, like this design by Allisa Jacobs, below right.

A hand mirror, whether antique or contemporary, is not only a memento of your wedding, but a lovely gift that she'll cherish for years to come. Colorful kimono-style robes make a great gifts, too. Wear them while getting ready, and you'll have the perfect attire that won't interfere with hair and makeup. Personalized bottles of their favorite kind of wine are unexpected and will be a big hit.

Another idea for your bridesmaids is a monthly box subscription. A box subscription is a delivery service for goods. You can give a gift subscription, prepaid in one-month, six-month, or one-year increments. You'll want to go online to see the huge variety available. I've seen boxes for DIY craft supplies, nail polish, beauty products, jewelry, and even specific clothing styles. When you sign her up for a subscription, she'll receive a box of new items every month (for as many months as you prepay). It's a fun twist on a traditional gift — and who doesn't love to get mail?

### GROOMSMEN

You can't go wrong with classic gifts for groomsmen, like a cigar cutter, a sterling-silver flask or tie tack, or a pair of cuff links. Check out KCowie online for custom made accessories. If you want to give them something a little more unique, try these modern gift ideas.

If beer is a favorite, consider a subscription club, where a different flavor of beer is sent to his door every month. Or, choose a DIY kit for making whiskey or beer. These kits are available online, and the recipes are easy to make at home. If you combine the kit with a party a few months before the wedding, the groomsmen can even make batches to enjoy on the wedding day.

Groomsmen will also appreciate gifts related to technology. Phone covers — see custom phone cases online at Carved — and laptop cases will work, or you could consider gift cards for buying items online, like e-books for a reading tablet or credits for purchasing digital music.

Groomsmen aren't necessarily expecting something extravagant. A game or funny book, an addition to an existing collection, and tickets to a sports event are all things they'd love to receive as a token of your appreciation.

Once you pick out the bridesmaid gift, think about what you'll give to the flower girl. She'll likely want something as cool as what you're giving the bridesmaids, so consider an age-appropriate item within the same category. A unique piece of jewelry she can wear for the wedding day and beyond is a fun gift. Make the piece extra special by customizing it with her monogram or initial, like these pendant necklaces left, by The Merriweather Council. You could also purchase a craft kit or a colorful bag or purse that looks similar to the bridesmaids'. Or, for a nostalgic alternative, you could buy her a few toys that you loved when you were her age.

Give the ring bearer a kid-friendly item like a game or a book. I've also seen ring bearers presented with a special "ring-bearer cape" to wear during the ceremony and then to take home. If he's into superheroes, this gift will probably make his entire year.

Both the flower girl and the ring bearer will need something fun to do while they are "off duty" at the wedding and during the reception. Give each of them a tote bag filled with entertaining goodies, such as a toy, a coloring book and crayons, a book of word puzzles, and candy.

## thoughtful extras

These are the little things that can make a big difference. Clear signage, meaningful touches, and gentle reminders are all appreciated by your guests.

If your ceremony and reception are in different locations, consider hiring a shuttle bus to take guests to and from the reception. This is especially helpful if your wedding is being held in a large downtown area, which might be difficult for some guests to navigate. Give guests a heads-up by placing a sign at the ceremony or writing a blurb in your wedding program. Be sure to include a list of shuttle departure times (both to and from the reception site).

A more luxurious option is a limousine bus, which can be used exclusively by your wedding party to travel to the ceremony, the photo location, and the reception.

## PROCESSION

Instead of tossing rice or seeds at the newlyweds, provide guests with silver or gold confetti poppers or noisemakers. Biodegradable confetti (which looks beautiful in the winter) is a modern-day alternative that breaks down naturally outdoors. Here is a fun bag design, above right, from Mavora Art and Design, for the confetti, check out Flower Fetti on Etsy.

## IN MEMORY OF

A sweet idea for honoring a loved one who has passed away is to place an "in memory of" sign on a chair, along with a framed photograph of the family member or friend.

## TECHNOLOGY

Do you love modern technology but cringe at the thought of cell phones and other electronic devices interrupting your wedding? Fear not. Ask guests to power down by posting a discreet sign at the entrance to your ceremony.

# The Attire

How will you dress your wedding crew? In this section, I'll share my favorite tips and styles for dressing the bride and groom — and all of their attendants. Let's begin with attire for the bride.

## the bride

As with other wedding themes, selecting the perfect urban-chic wedding dress has a lot to do with what looks best on you. Whether you prefer a strapless, halter, or sweetheart neckline, you'll want to look for a dress that suits your taste and personality. There's no definitive dress style for a contemporary bride; wearing what makes you happy is the number-one rule.

For a modern theme, however, you should avoid fabrics and styles that are strongly identified with bygone days. Instead of lace, look for a dress with pleats or plaits, or with minimal adornment. If you are planning a chic soiree and prefer a short dress, go for it. Want a long dress with an amazing train? It's really up to you.

What will you wear in your hair? A wedding veil is the classic choice, but it's not a requirement. If your wedding is full of glamour, consider a halo-like metallic headband instead. The unexpected pop of shine will make this accessory appear more modern than bohemian.

In past decades, it would be uncommon for a bride to wear something over her dress that wasn't made of lace or tulle. For an urban-chic wedding, though, a cardigan sweater or bolero will show off your unique style and keep you warm in cooler months.

It's also worth noting that for this theme, some brides opt to wear a wedding gown during the ceremony, and then change into a reception dress for the latter part of the festivities. This dress is typically white in color, short in length, and made of a more lightweight material, to ensure that the bride can dance the night away comfortably.

### JEWELRY & OTHER ACCESSORIES

An urban-chic wedding-dress style may be loosely defined, but your accessories should clearly reflect contemporary colors and trends. Creative, thoughtful accessorizing will ensure that your wedding-day look is unlike anyone else's.

For a modern wedding, less is more. Elegant accents like a minimal clutch purse and crystal drop earrings finish the look tastefully.

SHOES

There is no standard "modern" shoe you need to wear, so feel free to express your personal style. Consider coordinating your shoes with the palette and "mood" of the rest of your accessories, whether that means wearing traditional white pumps or a pair of polka-dotted heels. Bolder brides can opt for an extra dose of color in their shoes, especially if their wedding features black, white, and red.

Want to skip heels altogether? Wear sandals instead! A pair of metallic sandals is perfect for the contemporary bride-to-be.

## bridesmaids

When picking out bridesmaid dresses for an urban-chic wedding, consider your color palette and the silhouette of the dress. Short hems, up-to-date fabrics, and flattering necklines are ideal. For several reasons, I love the idea of the little black (or navy blue) bridesmaid dress. Most likely, every bridesmaid in your wedding party already has a black dress that she loves in her closet (and, if not, it gives her an excuse to go buy one). Also, everyone owns a pair of black shoes, whether flats or heels. Finally, black is sophisticated and timeless; it goes with everything and ties into any season of the year.

While classic black is a traditional choice, it can become more contemporary with a few minor tweaks. For instance, instead of long black dresses, go short. Rather than selecting one neckline for everyone, let each bridesmaid pick her favorite style of neckline, so that each dress looks slightly different but the overall look is still cohesive. There is also a special bridesmaid dress known as a convertible dress, which is one dress

that can be worn several ways; try Muse Bridal Wear or Dessy. To modernize the classic black dress even more, give each bridesmaid brightly colored baubles to wear around her neck.

Another way to make a bridesmaid dress more modern is with an interesting hemline. A scallop hem, high-low hem, or tulip skirt are a few examples.

Ombre is a style in which colors go from dark to light within the same color family. The ombre effect can be used throughout your wedding — even with your bridesmaid dresses. For instance, if you select blue, you might have one bridesmaid wearing navy, one in cobalt, and one in sky blue. Or, with a pink palette, you would see coral, hot pink, and blush.

## the groom

Much like choosing attire for the bride, comfort and personal preference should guide the selections for the groom. You won't go wrong with a classic suit, a vest, and a dress shirt.

Some contemporary weddings gravitate toward a black-and-white color palette, largely because it is chic and sophisticated. Another reason, though, is that it goes with everything and can be worn in any season of the year. One of my favorite ideas for this look is for the groom to pair a black suit with a white dress shirt and a bow tie.

Instead of opting for a solid tie, choose a modern print or pattern that coordinates with your color palette. Brightly colored plaid, for instance, will add definition to his style.

A beautiful silk tie is a way to introduce a contemporary color to a traditional look. Select a dramatic shade, like canary yellow, or opt for black or gray — always a sophisticated choice.

Prefer the look of a bow tie? Pair it with a beige or gray vest, a button-down shirt, and coordinating dress pants.

The groom can show off his individual style through fancy footwear. Choose something comfortable, like oxfords, and swap out the original laces for a pair in an eye-catching color that complements his tie.

## groomsmen

Give the groomsmen a hint of (partially hidden) color with an item in a modern pattern that coordinates with your decor, like argyle socks in unexpected shades of hot pink and light pink.

## ring bearer & flower girl

Once the groomsmen's attire has been selected, choose an outfit for the ring bearer. A tuxedo is a great choice, or you can go more informal with dress pants (like khakis), a dress shirt, a pair of suspenders, and a bow tie. Just make sure that he is comfortable.

The flower girl also doesn't have to wear something incredibly fancy — but she may want to be like one of the bridesmaids. If so, she can wear a dress whose color and fabric coordinates with the bridesmaids' outfits. Or, she can opt for a style all her own. Look for a flower-girl dress with a tulle skirt, for example, or a dress made of eco-friendly cotton, a modern material that will keep her looking cute and comfortable all day long. (Try Olive & Fern.)

# The Flowers

If you're looking for inspiration to determine the choice of flowers, look no further than your bridal gown. Your dress is your muse; it reflects your personal style and will be in harmony with other elements. All of the design details of your gown, from the color to the fabric, can serve as inspiration for your wedding bouquet (and your bridesmaids'), the boutonnieres, corsages, and more.

## bouquets

When it comes to wedding flowers, the bridal bouquet is the star. It dictates the colors and styles of the flowers that will be used for boutonnieres and corsages, ceremony decor, and reception centerpieces. Look for texture and interest — the flowers don't have to be perfectly matched, as long as they are unified with your theme. By the way, if you're afraid that a case of nerves may pop up unexpectedly, consider using some sprigs of an aromatic flower that can bring instant calm, like lavender.

For an urban-chic spin on traditional flowers, try an unexpected combination, such as succulents paired with white blooms and bright-yellow craspedia. To coordinate with your bouquet, bridesmaids can carry an all-yellow arrangement of craspedia.

If you prefer a nonfloral option (that's also a bit edgier), consider an origami bouquet (plus boutonnieres and corsages, too) made entirely from paper, like this stunning example from The Little Red Button, above right. Wrap the "stems" in a bright shade of fabric ribbon from your color palette.

Having a winter wedding? A December bouquet can be so much fun and an opportunity to bring your creative thinking into play. Flowers are not out of the question at this time of year, but there are lots of nonfloral and wonderfully scented options during this most joyous season: small pine boughs, cedar sprigs, juniper, and eucalyptus are a few.

Your wedding bouquet will be one of the most photographed details of your wedding. Hold it proudly, show it off, and get lots of pictures.

## boutonnieres

Boutonnieres and other floral elements will take a cue from your bridal bouquet. They are not the sideshow, but an all-important supporting cast.

A boutonniere is usually a single flower or a miniature cluster of flowers, and it's typically worn on the left lapel of both the groom and groomsmen during the wedding ceremony. Choose the dominant flower from your bouquet whether you've selected succulents, craspedia, paper origami flowers, or any other design. Then, simply add some greenery or an ornamental accent.

## corsages

People often think that a corsage harkens back to "the olden days." But don't let that notion stop you from pinning one on your mother as well as the groom's mother, and any other female guests that are important to you.

The corsage is larger than a boutonniere and includes more flowers or other accents. If roses will be part of your bouquet, small clusters of miniature or teacup roses are perfect, especially those that carry a lovely scent. Pin them directly on the left side of the dress or collar, below the shoulder line. Or corsage can be worn on the left wrist.

# The Reception

Deciding how to decorate the reception space is one of the most exciting parts of the wedding-planning process. I find it especially fun to decorate a modern wedding, since there are so many new and evolving trends to inspire me. How will you make your reception space stand out from any other? In this section, I'll show you how it's done!

## the venue

Inside, outside, uptown, or downtown there are lots of options for an urban wedding reception. If you plan to have the reception at the same site as the ceremony, you can use strategic decorations to transform an area into a reception space.

The quintessential city party space has got to be a rooftop. Whether it's a hotel or an event center, you can't go wrong. The skyline, sunset, moon and stars, and sheer vibrancy of the urban setting make a perfect backdrop.

Or, your reception could take place in a private area of a nightclub, complete with a stage for a live band to perform.

This tastefully renovated factory, above left, features a place for guests to mingle admist mid-century furniture, a perfect counterpoint to the exposed brick and the amazing windows.

## escort cards & more

When guests arrive at your reception, most will either make a beeline to the bar or go straight to their seats. Ensure that they can find their table assignments quickly by providing an escort-card table or similar display. Opt for cards with a simple design and clear, easy-to-read type.

Make your escort cards really stand out with unexpected accents, like glitter. Here is a sparkling example by Hoopla Love, below left.

One of my favorite alternatives is to make escort cards from paint chips. Take a colorful assortment of paint chips and write a guest's name and table number on each one. Use clothespins to arrange them along a clothesline, so that guests can unpin their chips and find their tables.

## TABLE NUMBERS

Once your guests grab an escort card, they'll need to be able to locate their specific table. Make it easy by displaying a number at each table. For a modern twist on traditional numbering, consider these fun ideas. Instead of labeling with numbers, give your tables quirky names. Use places you've frequented as a couple; different types of wine or beer; or your favorite books, movies, bands, or movie stars. Or, simply assign each table a specific color.

## PLACE CARDS

If you don't have assigned seating, place cards aren't required (since guests can sit at any seat at their designated table). However, if you want a specific seating plan, place cards are a must. Contemporary place cards that coordinate with your wedding stationery (invitations and enclosures) are an easy addition to any table setting. You can make your own with a stamp, an ink pad, and folded tent cards.

## decor

Let your guests know that they've arrived at the right place! Distinguish the entrance to the reception area with a bold, personalized accent. Some of my favorite ideas are oversized monograms, custom silhouettes in your likenesses, or a personalized welcome sign placed on an easel near the entrance. Want to go in a different direction, more toward swanky? Try these "metal" letters sprayed with metallic paint and then dipped in silver glitter. Using lightweight cardstock makes them able to be hung anywhere.

### SIGNS

Direct guests to different areas of your reception space by using chalkboard signs with hand lettering. Using hot glue, attach each small chalkboard (available at any craft store) to a wooden dowel. Place the signs in a large vase or bucket, such as a galvanized pail filled with brightly colored shredded paper for added pop.

If you're planning a modern wedding with a watercolor theme, make your own decorative signs, using lyrics from favorite songs or other meaningful quotes. Prop each sign on a table, and complete the display with framed photos of the wedding couple.

### HANGING DECOR

There are a few ways to incorporate hanging decor into an urban-chic wedding. One technique is to use garlands. Garlands can decorate your walls, draw attention to your cake table or guest-book table, and even dress up your head table. Garlands for a modern wedding are typically made of paper fringe, paper tassels, or small paper or fabric pom-poms (made into garlands by stringing twine through the poms with a needle and clear thread).

The ceiling is a perfect spot for placing eye-catching decorations. For instance, an assortment of big, bold, colorful paper lanterns creates a dramatic dance floor.

If you've chosen a more minimalist, all-white color palette, use just a few white lanterns, spaced apart, and fill in the gaps with white string lights.

To create a gorgeous glow above your outdoor reception space, hang prelit paper lanterns in muted tones.

Don't overlook another surface that can be decorated: the floor! You can modernize the dance floor by applying a removable decal with your monogram. Or, use a projector to beam your names onto the center of the dance floor.

## table decor

For your reception tables, use table runners in modern prints and patterns, rather than a solid color, to underscore your theme. Some examples include chevrons, a preppy lattice print, a Greek key pattern, houndstooth, ikat, scrolls, paisley, or plaid, just to name a few. Use a white tablecloth underneath to ensure a striking contrast.

If your reception tables are beautiful as is, consider using a patterned table runner without an underlying tablecloth. Then, accent the tables with simple decor — like succulents, illuminated lamps, and brightly colored candleholders — rather than an overwhelming centerpiece arrangement.

While succulents can look lovely in nearly any wedding theme, these small green plants are especially appropriate for decorating an urban-chic wedding reception. Why? They're low profile, uniquely shaped, and tastefully understated.

If you prefer a bit more glamour and glitz, outfit your reception tables with sequins. A sequined tablecloth, sequined table runner, or even sequined chair backs will glam up your gala instantly. If you are using a sweetheart table, make a pair of simple yet swanky chair sashes by using a roll of elastic sequin trimming. Select gold, silver, or black trimming, to coordinate with your decor; cut about a foot and a half of trim per chair. Hot glue a strip of fabric behind each piece of trim, for durability. Once the glue is dry, tie a sequined sash in a bow on the back of each chair.

## CENTERPIECES

For a minimalist centerpiece (skipping the flowers), fill clear, cylindrical glass vases with water and add a floating candle to each one. Group them en masse at the center of your table. To add a table number, affix a number sticker to one of the glass vases.

If you're using craspedia in your wedding bouquet, incorporate it into your centerpieces. Just a few craspedia stems in an elegant vase will do, paired with candles and small plants.

Make your own reusable "green" centerpieces with succulents, cacti, or other hardy plants. Tightly group a handful of plants in a wooden planter box, and place a box at the center of each table. Add a table number to complete the look.

After the wedding, give away the plants to loved ones as favors, or bring them home to plant in your own garden.

## guest book

Want an updated version of the traditional guest book? Use photographs from recent travels, your courtship, or events from the last year and create a book. (There are many photo services online, such as Snapfish.) Print your names on the front, along with your wedding date. Include white pages throughout where guests can sign their names and express their well wishes.

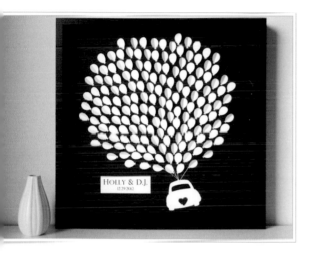

Here is another guest-book alternative: have each guest sign his or her name on a small paper heart or balloon. After the wedding, the pieces can be assembled into a 3-D work of art — like this beautiful example, left, by Suzy Shoppe — that can be framed and displayed proudly in your home.

If you're planning to work some origami into your wedding, buy or make an origami crane for every guest. Sew a loop of ribbon onto each crane, and place them in a basket on the guest-book table. Post an invitation for each guest to sign a crane and then hang it onto a "wishing tree" (like a tabletop manzanita tree) for good luck.

## photo booth

If you're having a photo booth at your wedding, make the photos even more memorable by incorporating the guests' snapshots into your guest book. Among your photo-booth props, include a large, hand-held chalkboard and pieces of chalk (or chalk pens). Each guest can write a message on the board, sign his or her name, and have a photograph taken with it. After the wedding, assemble all the photos and turn them into a scrapbook or photo album. To instantly modernize the booth, decorate it with a colorful backdrop; visit a craft store for fabric or rolls of paper that have a geometric pattern or a vibrant print.

Another option is to have a favorite photo of the two of you enlarged and matted in white. Rest the photo on an easel at a guest-book table. Place a small pail of pens and a sign beside the easel, asking guests to sign on the matting. After the wedding, your photo will already be matted — including the well wishes and signatures of loved ones — and ready to frame and display.

## the sweetheart table

In a more formal, traditional wedding, the bride and groom sit with the wedding party at a head table. For a urban-chic wedding, I recommend a "sweetheart" table instead. A sweetheart table is a small table with two chairs for the two of you to sit together.

## wedding favors

What will you give to guests as a token of your appreciation? Here are some ideas to spark your creativity.

A favorite type of candy — always a crowd-pleaser — can be placed in small boxes that are embellished with origami hearts. Planning a candy buffet? Make your own take-home treat containers, using white or brown paper bags, stamped with geometric designs and your wedding date. Invite guests to fill them up with their favorite colorful candies.

Having a sweets bar instead? Give each guest a take-away treat, like a brightly colored candy apple in a convenient, to-go package.

Succulent plants, which cost a few dollars apiece, make a great gift that your guests are sure to enjoy. Place a succulent plant in a wooden box or planter; tie a tag around the succulent and include instructions on care. Place one boxed plant at each guest's table setting, so that it doubles as decor.

Soap has been given as a favor many times before, but rarely with this modern twist: present guests with soap in a geometric shape, such as a large diamond tucked inside a cleverly decorated box, like this unique favor from Vice & Velvet, right.

Another fun idea is a pin-back button, custom made with a motif from your wedding. These buttons, right, were created by Big Yellow Dog Designs.

While this idea applies to any wedding theme, a donation in lieu of favors is an increasingly popular favor option. If there's a special cause or charity that is significant to you and your groom, donate money to the organization instead of buying favors for guests. Provide a card at each guest's seat that says, "In lieu of favors, a donation has been made to [the name of the organization]." You can also include a brief summary explaining why the charity is meaningful to you and what services it provides.

If you have a photo booth at your reception, let guests take home an instant photo as a favor. For storing their keepsake, provide a clear photo sleeve at each seat. Include a note that invites your guests to visit the photo booth.

## entertainment

For an urban-chic wedding, dancing is usually the number-one choice for keeping guests entertained, whether the music is played by a live band or a deejay. In this theme, though, there are additional ways you can wow your guests. If your wedding venue allows, arrange for fireworks to be launched after dark. Or, hire a caricature artist to sketch guests, a comedian to make them laugh, a magician to impress them with illusion, or a celebrity impersonator to keep them wondering.

Will kids be in attendance? Provide coloring books, crayons, and other enticing items to keep them busy at their table before or after dinner is served.

## the cake

For a minimalist look, order a cake iced with fondant, which creates a smooth, seamless surface. Embellish the tiers of your cake with thin strips of ribbon and a small, simple fondant flower. Create a slightly industrial effect with a cake stand or pedestal forged from metal.

If bold is more your style, use a pattern or print to turn your cake into a statement piece. A chevron wedding cake is one example; for an additional modern touch, use a monogram on the top tier and skip the cake topper.

If you prefer a cake topper, however, opt for something distinctly contemporary, like custom bobbleheads or figurines that are made in your image. (One online resource is Dream Cake Toppers.) Other suggestions include a single felt heart on a stick, placed directly into the top tier of your cake; animals dressed in wedding attire to resemble the bride and groom; and a zinc monogram letter, like this engraved example from Julie the Fish Designs, below right.

If your wedding decor has a particular theme, let it guide your cake-topper selection. If you've been decorating with origami paper, for instance, opt for a cake topper made of origami cranes, or consider bride-and-groom figurines made from specially folded paper, like this one from Lulu's Little Shop, opposite, top right.

If a traditional wedding cake doesn't appeal to you, consider a modern variation instead. Candy buffets and delicious desserts like cake pops and pie pops are just a few options. Cupcakes are another popular, bite-size treat that guests will surely enjoy. You can display cupcakes on top of a cupcake tower, which is crafted from different levels of wood. To make the cupcakes even more enticing, set up a custom cupcake-topping station, stocked with sprinkles, chocolate chips, and other tempting confections.

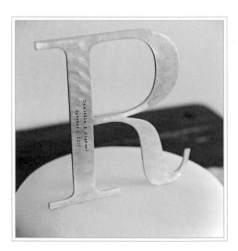

Have you heard of a "groom's cake"? It's a special cake that is ordered and designed by the bride as a surprise for the groom. If you're considering a groom's cake, choose a theme that is all about him, such as his favorite professional sports team, college mascot, or hobby.

## grand exit

Make a grand exit to your getaway car with a confetti toss. I recommend using biodegradable confetti that is water soluble, eco-friendly, and non-harmful to birds and animals. Plus, since it breaks down naturally, you won't have to clean it up. Make sure it's lightweight so your photographer has ample time to capture the moment on film. One place to find biodegradable confetti is Save On Crafts.

# Resources

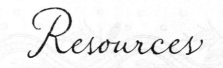

Page 141
Daydream Prints / www.etsy.com/shop/daydreamprints
Serendipity Beyond Design / www.etsy.com/shop/beyonddesign
Jen Simpson Design / www.jensimpsondesign.com

Page 142
Hoopla Love / www.etsy.com/shop/hooplalove

Page 146
Scissor Mill / www.etsy.com/shop/ScissorMill

Page 147
Chiavari / www.chiavarichairs.com
Sparkle Soiree / www.etsy.com/shop/SparkleSoiree

Page 148
Little Blue Feathers /www.etsy.com/shop/littlebluefeathers
Flower Fetti / www.etsy.com/shop/Flowerfetti
LV Woodworks / www.etsy.com/shop/LVwoodworks

Page 149
Hoopla Love / www.etsy.com/shop/hooplalove

Page 150
Allisa Jacobs / www.allisajacobs.com

page 151
KCowie / www.etsy.com/shop/KCowie
Carved / www.carved.com/

Page 152
The Merriweather Council / www.merriweathercouncil.com

Page 153
Mavora Art & Design / www.etsy.com/shop/mavora
Flower Fetti / www.etsy.com/shop/Flowerfetti

Page 158
Muse Bridal Wear / www.musebridalwear.com
The Dessy Group / www.dessy.com

Page 160
Olive & Fern / www.etsy.com/shop/oliveandfern

Page 162
The Little Red Button / www.etsy.com/shop/thelittleredbutton

Page 165
Hoopla Love / www.etsy.com/shop/hooplalove

Page 171
Snapfish / www.Snapfish.com
Suzy Shoppe / www.etsy.com/shop/suzyshoppe

Page 172
Vice & Velvet / www.etsy.com/shop/viceandvelvet

Page 173
Big Yellow Dog Designs / www.etsy.com/shop/bigyellowdogdesigns

Page 174
Dream Cake Toppers / www.DreamCakeToppers.com
Julie the Fish Designs / www.etsy.com/shop/juliethefish
Lulu's Little Shop / www.etsy.com/shop/luluslittleshop

Page 175
Save On Crafts / www.save-on-crafts.com

# Free Spirit

I get it: you don't fuss over frills or swoon over soft palettes and colorful peonies. Maybe you don't want to do what everyone else does for their wedding, and, as a result, you're looking for something different. If you're going against the herd and you don't want to play by the rules, then this chapter is written for you. From slightly unconventional to downright unorthodox, there's bound to be a style here that suits you best.

# Invitations & More

No matter the wedding theme, you'll want an invitation suite that expresses your personal style — and when you're a free spirit, there are lots of options. From the beginning, you'll want to convey your unconventional attitude by selecting nontraditional save-the-date cards and invitations. In this section, you'll find ideas for a broad spectrum of offbeat invitations, including some subcategories you may not have considered.

## invitations & save the dates

When I began researching this chapter, I went to my readers first. At Emmaline Bride, we cover lots of wedding topics — but several "offbeat" themes kept surfacing and were obviously more popular. Here are the free-spirited themes that I think will remain popular well into the future.

**Computer games** • Games of any type are great for bringing like-minded people together. But fans of 8-bit computer games are also especially fond of applying this retro style to popular culture, in everything from apparel to posters to music. It's an aesthetic that's very appealing, and it makes a fun, clever subgenre for a free-spirit wedding. M³ and Co., above left, has managed just the right touch in this invitation design.

**Steampunk** • This genre of science fiction, termed in the late 1980s, is fueled by creativity and a big imagination. Aficionados of steampunk take great pride in transforming bits and pieces of everyday mechanical items into something elegant. For your invitation design, this may mean using elements from the Victorian era, mixed with futuristic typefaces and graphics. In the design above right, there's a Machine Age look that's been updated to the 21st century. The invitation concept from Ruff House Art, below, includes hints of the Victorian era (with the moustache and top hat), combined with eccentric typefaces and a graphically pleasing color palette.

**Graphic novels** • Are you and your hubby-to-be fans of retro style comic book heroes or anime? Are you writers or illustrators who are inspired by graphic novels? If so, you can have the most fun when you let a visual style or a storyline guide your theme.

Geek chic • A geek can most easily be defined as a person who is absolutely devoted to something, whether it's dinosaurs, robots, music, or math. Many couples meet for the first time because of their shared passion, and the paper-product designs for your wedding can express the significance of that enthusiasm.

I love this fun design from Crafty Pie Press, above left, featuring preppy eyeglass frames that are de rigueur for a bonafide geek look.

An interesting collection of vinyl records or a love of prehistoric beasts can equally inspire and inform your invites. The design from LetterBoxInk, below right, uses replicas of 45 records and a concert ticket to create the perfect touch for this retro-inspired wedding.

You get the idea: the opportunities are as big as your imagination, and these subgenres are just some possibilities for a wedding in the free-spirit theme. Inspiration can come from just about everywhere — a color palette, hobby, or anything that you both agree is pretty awesome can equal a theme. All that matters is that it is a genuine expression of your love for each other paired with a desire for some whimsy and personal expression.

The theme of "us" is also rich with ideas. The invitation from Sparkvites opposite, tells the story of the couple, how they met, and their eventual engagement. The designers created an inviting invitation — I wouldn't be able to say "no" to this event!

## PLEASE REPLY

TARA AND FELIPE ARE THROWING AN/AN _____
*ADJECTIVE*

PARTY TO CELEBRATE THEIR WEDDING, AND ARE INVITING YOU

BECAUSE YOU HAVE PLAYED SUCH A/AN _____
*ADJECTIVE*

ROLE IN THEIR JOURNEY TOGETHER.

_____
*YOUR NAME(S)*

_____  BE THERE TO _____
*WILL OR WILL NOT*                                              *VERB*

WE CAN'T WAIT TO DANCE TO _____
*SONG REQUEST*

AND SEE THE HAPPY COUPLE _____
*VERB*

WE WISH THEM MANY YEARS OF HAPPINESS AND _____
*NOUN*

## DIRECTIONS

**MARTY LEONARD COMMUNITY CHAPEL**
3131 SANGUINET STREET
FORT WORTH, TEXAS 76107

**JOE T GARCIA'S LA FUENTES**
2201 NORTH COMMERCE
FORT WORTH, TEXAS 76164

## REGISTRY

### WE ARE REGISTERED AT

**HOME DEPOT**
7830 NORTH FREEWAY
FORT WORTH, TX

**HOME DEPOT**
AT 121 & MID CITIES BLVD
EULESS, TX

**THE CONTAINER STORE**
IN STORES
AND ONLINE

# The Ceremony

When brides ask what type of location to consider for their unconventional wedding, the answer is: almost anywhere. However, I do recommend one rule when looking for a venue: it should reflect you as a couple. I've read many stories about engaged couples trying to top the last couple in terms of weird or unusual places to tie the knot. While it can be fun to receive notoriety, a wedding is a significant union between two lovers, and the place you choose to join together should be meaningful to both of you.

## the venue

An aquarium has recently become one of my favorite wedding locations. Who knew? That location hadn't occurred to me, but of course it makes perfect sense, as does a zoo, a natural-history museum, a bookstore, or even an underwater site. I've had a lot of fun researching the free-spirit theme, and now I know that nearly any place is a possible venue, as long as the organization or the person in charge is willing to make it available to you.

An aquarium makes a quietly stunning ceremony and reception location, with its soft lighting a backdrop of blue water with schools of brightly colored fish swimming by. Another benefit is that it's a year-round venue.

Likewise, a similar location (recommended for warm weather only) is a zoo. If you admire animals, are adventurous, and prefer to marry near or inside your favorite exhibit, this is the spot for you. I've seen some beautiful weddings that have taken place within special exhibits, like a butterfly house or an aviary — love-bird central!

Are you an avid theatergoer or movie lover? Consider renting a theater for your wedding ceremony and reception. Depending on your specific interest, you could deck it out with a *Star Wars*, *The Wizard of Oz*, or Shakespearean theme. Other locations to consider are a library, a botanical garden, or even a brewery.

A children's museum, like the Marbles Kids Museum in Raleigh, North Carolina, is another interesting place to tie the knot, as well as the Museum of Life + Science in Durham, above left. The Marble Museum features a large marble wall, below left, which can act as your ceremony focal point.

Of course, there's nothing like an outdoor wedding on a perfect summer's day (just be prepared with bug spray, sunscreen, and protection from the elements). Colorful signage like this, above right, can make a fun focal point for an outside wedding.

## seating & aisle decor

How will guests be seated at your wedding? If you're getting married at a location that typically hosts large gatherings, the venue will likely provide the aisle seating, as well as tables and chairs for the reception. (Honestly, many venues will arrange just about anything you may need, indoors or out, from decor to catering.) If your wedding is in an unusual out-of-the-way place or a private location, such as your own backyard, you will probably need to rent or borrow these items yourselves.

At a free-spirit-style backyard wedding I once attended, the couple gathered up an array of wildly eclectic chairs, stools, and benches from thrift stores and friends providing comfortable seating for guests in an unexpected (and artistic) variety of rows. I've seen other options, too, from garden benches to beanbag chairs — even blankets on the ground. Colorful sheets can cover long benches or hay bales, which are surprisingly comfortable and easy to arrange.

Whether you're marrying indoors or out, aisle decor can define the ceremony space and make it your own. For a whimsical wedding, make large paper or felt pom-poms in vibrant colors and attach them to chairs along the aisle, using clear tape. Similarly, paper pinwheels can be constructed from brightly colored scrapbook paper and adhered to chairs with a bit of clear tape. A bunting banner, made from fabric scraps and twine and stretched from one end of the aisle to the other, will add a playful touch to the aisle design. Opt for bold, punchy pops of color that complement your wedding bouquet or color palette.

Giant dinosaur footprints can make their way up the aisle, or a handful of parasols — particularly perfect for a steampunk wedding — can be lined along the aisle in lieu of flowers or other decor.

## vows & readings

When you're planning a nontraditional wedding, conventional vows may be one area of the ceremony you'd like to change, especially if you feel that the customary verbiage is not a reflection of who you are as a couple. The promises you make to each other are personal, so consider taking some time to write your own vows. It's not as daunting as you may think. You can seek help from family members or friends, and even online. Look for excerpts or quotes that speak to both of you, or even jokes can be incorporated.

If you're not a sentimental or overly serious couple, write vows that reveal your silly side. For instance, "I vow to let you hog the remote, as long as you always get rid of the spiders." You'll want to include some quirky quips, but try not to skip the sweet emotions entirely.

If you decide to have readings, they can be read by your officiant, you and your spouse, or anyone at the celebration. Presenting a meaningful poem or passage from a significant book is a powerful way to personalize your day, and even more so when a piece is chosen and read by a family member, guest, or someone from your wedding party.

A ceremony program is the perfect place to include the source of the readings, so that guests can refer to it after the wedding.

## nontraditional traditions

Rituals vary greatly with a free-spirit wedding, mostly because there are no rules. If you like a particular custom, follow it. If you don't, drop it. It's as simple as that. Here are a few of my favorite alternatives to traditional practices during the ceremony.

A handfasting ceremony is an ancient ritual that was performed in Scotland and Ireland. Before the rings are exchanged, the bride and groom cross arms and join hands in a figure eight, which is a sign of infinity and their lasting commitment to each other. The officiant then "binds" the couple's hands with a ribbon or cord. Traditionally, handfasting lasts for "one year and one day" after that — the couple can "reevaluate" their relationship.

In another alternative practice, the bride opts to walk down the aisle alone, rather than being "given away" to her future spouse. Or she may be accompanied by her mother, a sister, or her maid of honor.

Have you heard of a ring warming? Although I wouldn't consider it to be exclusive to the free-spirit style, it's a lovely tradition for a bride and her groom. In this ritual, the rings are passed amongst the guests. Each guest makes a silent blessing or prayer for the couple, and then passes the rings to the next person. (Some couples place the rings in a special bag or attach them to a pillow, which can alleviate any worry of rings being dropped.) Once the rings have been passed to all of the guests, they are returned to the officiant, and the exchange of vows (and rings) begins.

I once saw a ritual that was similar to the ring warming, but it took place at a beach wedding. Instead of blessing rings, each guest was given a seashell or pebble to hold. After the ceremony, the guests walked to the shoreline with the newlyweds,

made a blessing for them, and tossed their seashells or pebbles into the water.

Some couples are dropping the rings altogether and are having "rings" tattooed on their ring fingers instead. Or, they are selecting an alternative to a diamond ring (a gemstone or pearl, for instance).

Can't decide whether to follow the custom of not seeing each other until the ceremony? Try this: a partial first look. Standing on either side of a door allows you to hold hands and talk to your fiancé, while still saving the big reveal for the ceremony.

## flower girl & ring bearer

Instead of tossing petals and holding a ring pillow, the flower girl and ring bearer can walk down the aisle carrying something more unexpected. For instance, a lightsaber, a charming "Here Comes the Bride" banner, or giant round balloons from Koyal Wholesale are just a few ideas. (If you're going to use balloons, make sure they're the oversized round ones, to avoid the appearance of a birthday party.

A fun idea is for the flower girl and ring bearer to join forces and each hold a pennant. The ones above, from Betawife, are inspired by the famous scene from *The Empire Strikes Back*, between Princess Leia and Han Solo.

The flower girl could carry a pinwheel, which is even more fun when it's oversized. If you have a dinosaur theme, the ring bearer could carry a figurine of his favorite

dinosaur. Or, he can carry an action figure — from *Transformers* or *Star Wars*, for instance — down the aisle. You can attach the rings, or give them to your best man to hold. If you're planning a Halloween-themed or gothic wedding, consider a small box with a hinge to contain the rings. If you're going the steampunk route, line the inside of the box with black lace or felt for an added effect. Or, search on Etsy for a few custom-made options.

Need a secret spot to store the rings? Have the ring bearer carry them down the aisle inside a favorite book, particularly if you're planning a literary-themed wedding. Inside the book, carve into the pages to create a "pocket" where the rings can sit. Or, use a hollow book (found at craft stores) instead.

## wedding-party gifts

What will your wedding party receive as gifts? While a cuff-link set or a flask seem like traditional go-to gifts for groomsmen, they aren't out of place here. Instead of formal cuff links, give groomsmen superhero-inspired ones, above left. Online, look at Erica B. Studios on Etsy and Kustom Kufflinks.

Steampunk-style cuff links, made of metal and real watch gears, is another option, above right.

A flask is never boring, especially when it reflects your central theme. For a steampunk wedding, look for a leather-wrapped flask or one embellished with gears. For the gamer, look for a Zelda Triforce emblem on a flask. Fan of literary works? A Harry Potter enthusiast would enjoy a flask with a Hogwarts House symbol or a special box set of the book collection.

If your wedding revolves around a favorite TV show, look for related items, like a TARDIS mug for a *Doctor Who* fan. Love *Star Wars*? A Darth Vader beer glass can be used prior to the wedding (and will become a keepsake for his bar).

Don't buy the same gift for all bridesmaids, when each has a different personality. For instance, one bridesmaid might prefer a gift certificate for a manicure and pedicure, while another might want a gift certificate for a bookstore, favorite movie house, or a custom clutch purse. Another way to gift your bridesmaids is by covering a wedding-related expense, like makeup and hair before the ceremony, a hotel room for after the reception, new shoes, or part of the cost of the bridesmaid dress.

## transportation

Whether you're arriving at the ceremony or driving from the ceremony to the reception, your transportation can also be a bit quirky or offbeat. If a limousine isn't in your future, consider renting something unique — like a vintage covertible, an old VW bus, or a big, old yellow school bus that can transport your wedding party to and from the festivities.

# The Attire

Are you a bride who is considering wearing a dress based on *Doctor Who*'s TARDIS machine? Maybe you're thinking of a steampunk-style gown with a velvet corset and a striped satin skirt? Or, do you want to break out of the ordinary and have fun, but not look like you're going to a costume party? You're in luck — I've got lots of ideas for either scenario.

## the bride

In a free-spirit wedding, dare to be different! A short wedding dress in white; a sleeveless, hot-pink dress; a black, gothic-style gown; a gown with brightly colored tights underneath; and a dyed petticoat are a few options for are putting a personal twist on the traditional bridal ensemble. When you're looking for your dress, pick the style that suits and flatters you best. It's your wedding, and your look is completely up to you. And remember, your offbeat wedding doesn't have to be nontraditional in every aspect, only in the areas you want it to be.

You can always add accessories to your gown (or to your overall look) to express your theme or personality. A bold floral sash or jeweled belt, for example, will instantly enhance your look.

If your style is more Victorian or steampunk, look for a lace gown and pair it with a leather dress belt. Instead of a veil, the bride might don a top hat or feathers, or even carry a parasol in a rich, colorful hue.

There are many other alternatives to the traditional veil. Whether you wear a feathery hair comb, a funky hair clip, or a bridal hat, be sure that it ties into your theme. For instance, I saw a wedding where the bride and groom added quirky pop (or soda, depending on where you may live) caps into their decor, which totally reflected their offbeat personalities. The bride even incorporated a bottle cap into her floral hair accessory, below left, along with a burst of purple to represent her favorite flavor, grape.

If you're planning a gothic or "Day of the Dead"–style wedding, a black wedding gown might be your preferred choice. Or, a white gown with black accents (like a black floral sash, or a corset-style gown with black satin ribbons lining the back) would work well, too. Instead of white heels, wear black; instead of a white veil, wear a black birdcage veil or a black feathery hair clip.

Find other ways to accessorize with thematic elements. For example, you could embroider a charming, robot-themed handkerchief and wrap it around your bouquet handle.

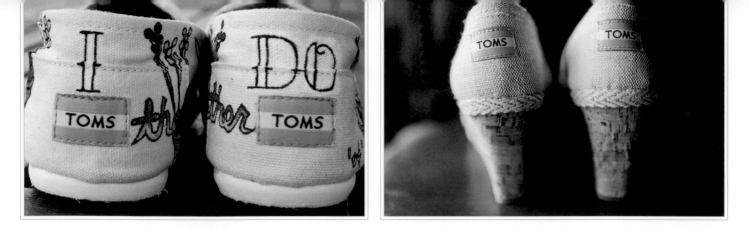

What will you wear on your feet? Bridal shoes in white or ivory are classic, but as a free-spirit bride, you're probably looking for something a bit more exciting. Patterned tights in an array of colors can be found at most department stores or online at a site such as Zappos. If you're looking to wear flats, consider hand painting your wedding date and names on a pair of TOMs shoes.

For a gothic-style wedding, black-lace heels, flats, or barefoot sandals are a few options, while leather boots, lace-up boots, or Victorian pumps are fitting for a steampunk wedding. Or, you can never go wrong with a pair of shoes in your favorite color, regardless of the theme.

## bridesmaids

For an offbeat wedding, skip the traditional bridesmaid dresses and opt for something a little more fun. Ask your girls to pick a dress within specific shade (provide a swatch as a visual), with differing patterns and necklines. For instance, one of your bridesmaids could select a blue halter-style dress with white polka dots, while another might select a strapless dress with a striped pattern. Or, you can forgo dresses altogether and select shorts or skorts in your color palette.

Want to give total freedom to your bridesmaids? Tell them to wear any dress they love in any color, which solidifies a nonconforming look and guarantees they'll actually wear their dresses again (since each one picked it out or already had it in her closet). If you want some aspect of their look to correspond, buy gloves, jewelry, or coordinating hair accessories for them to wear. For a steampunk-style wedding, for instance, a long strand of pearls, a feather hair comb,or a pair of elbow-length white gloves would help them standout as bridesmaids.

If you're planning a retro-music or rockabilly wedding, pick 1950s frocks with colorful vintage patterns, short hemlines, and sweetheart necklines. For a gothic-themed wedding, ask the bridesmaids to wear a black lacy dress, and let them decide what style of neckline and length to wear. Give them matching necklaces, and ask them to wear black shoes of any style.

In a free-spirit wedding, it's fairly common for the bride and groom to elect a best woman (instead of "man") or a man of honor (instead of "Maid") — more commonly known as an honor attendant — to go against tradition. For attire, the best woman would wear the same style of dress as the bridesmaids, but perhaps in a different color to coordinate with the groomsmen. Or, her bouquet might match the boutonnieres instead of the bridesmaids' bouquets.

Prefer a more offbeat (and menswear-inspired) look? The best woman can wear a solid black dress with a bow-tie accent and shoes that take a cue from the men (like an oxford-style pair of heels). For a feminine look, you can craft the bow tie into a necklace she can wear, rather than pinning it onto her dress, or you could buy a necklace with a bow-tie pendant.

The male honor attendant can wear the same attire as the groomsmen; however, his tie or boutonniere would coordinate with the bridesmaids' bouquets.

## groom & groomsmen

What will the groom and his groomsmen wear? For this wedding theme, tuxedos take a backseat to casual options, such as jeans and button-down shirts with jackets, short-sleeved dress shirts and (offbeat) ties, or dress pants and vests.

When you're considering attire, first think about what your groom is most comfortable wearing. For instance, if he prefers to dress in a pair of khakis with a button-down shirt, go with that — and maybe add a colorful bow tie.

Going bold? A patterned suit with a whimsical print and a coordinating bow tie fit right into this theme. Going geek? Relaxed khaki pants or shorts, a button-down shirt, a tie, and suspenders would work. If you're having a carnival-themed wedding, a bow tie, a striped shirt, and suspenders are a winning combination.

If you're not willing to dive into totally off-the-wall ideas, use a few unexpected accents instead. A traditional suit in gray, black, or beige, with a white button-down shirt and a coordinating tie, looks great on every man. Swap the dress socks for a pair of eccentric patterned or themed socks, like ones with the TARDIS from *Doctor Who*. Or, he can don a fedora to look slightly offbeat but still in keeping with a more traditional dress code.

If you're having a superhero-themed wedding, for instance, the groomsmen can wear Superman socks underneath their dress pants as a playful way to underscore the theme — and this makes for a memorable photograph.

A patterned shirt and a quirky necktie under a neutral vest is an unusual combination, but it fits in remarkably well at an eccentric, slightly unconventional wedding.

Want your groomsmen to be completely comfortable? Jeans, a sweater (in either a matching or coordinating shade, for cohesion), and a pair of sneakers (think Converse) will suit them. Add a boutonniere to each groomsman's sweater, so that he isn't mistaken for a guest.

A man's shoes say a lot about his style, so think outside the box on dress shoes for the groom. What does he like to wear on a regular basis? That can clue you in on what he might like to wear for the wedding. For instance, leather boots (like Dr. Martens), wing-tipped dress shoes, oxfords, or even saddle shoes are a few offbeat selections your groom will love to wear again.

Finally, don't forget to incorporate quirky accessories, like brightly colored sunglasses frames for the entire wedding party to wear.

# flower girl & ring bearer

When you're selecting ring-bearer attire, use the groomsmen's wardrobe as a guide. Typically, the ring bearer should wear a miniature version of the groomsmen's outfits.

The same rule applies to the flower girl. If the bridesmaids are wearing *Star Wars*-inspired frocks, for example, the flower girl should follow suit (in an age-appropriate version). Of course, the flower girl can always be dressed in something slightly different, such as a tulle dress, if you prefer.

# *The Flowers*

In a traditional wedding, flowers are everywhere: the bride carries them, her bridesmaids have their own bouquets, and centerpieces are overflowing with fragrant, full-bloom floral arrangements. For an a free-spirit wedding, though, floral alternatives are often the norm. In this section, I'll share some of my favorite offbeat ideas.

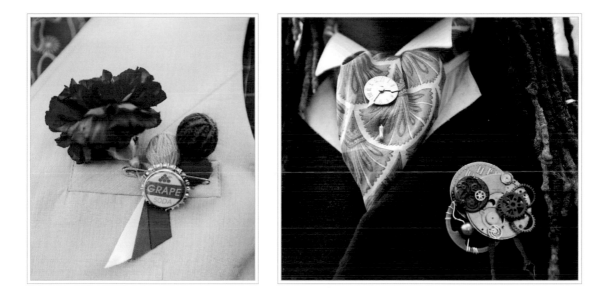

## boutonnieres

A handmade boutonniere for the groom and groomsmen can include a flower stem, small balls of yarn, ribbon, and a grape-soda bottle cap, as seen above left.

For a steampunk wedding, you'll want to jump right into gear with a mechanically inspired piece for the groom, such as the one in the photograph above right. Look for other ideas at When Geeks Wed and on Etsy, the shops She Wore White and Michelle's Clay Creations.

In the photograph above left, the groom is sporting a dyed deep-blue rose bud — as are his groomsmen — which coordinates with his bow tie, the bride's bouquet, and the dresses of the bridal party (see the photo on page 197).

Handmade boutonnieres could also incorporate black feathers or tulle, paper-flower rosettes made from the pages of your favorite book, or action figures from a movie you both love. Or, add some comic-book "POW!" with a boutonniere made from a few layers of hand-cut felt in different colors, finished with embroidery accents.

## bouquets

For a steampunk bride, consider carrying an arrangement made of creatively twisted metal and timepieces fashioned to look like a bouquet.

A favorite nonfloral option that offers plenty of color and will never wilt is the paper bouquet. Available in any color combination under the sun, a paper bouquet (see the opposite page) is perfect for the nontraditional bride who wants a bouquet that's made to last forever.

If you are a quirky and crafty bride, create your own bouquet from balls of yarn, polka-dotted fabric flowers, button "stems," ribbons, and vintage handkerchiefs.

Another option — to coordinate with the flower girl, too — is for bridesmaids to carry big paper roses, oversized lollipops, or giant pinwheels. Is your wedding literary themed? Invite bridesmaids (and the flower girl) to carry a favorite book down the aisle.

# The Reception

Are you looking for ideas for your free-spirit, unconventional wedding reception? What about a breakfast-themed reception, featuring everyone's favorite cereals, made-to-order omelettes, and hot-off-the-grill pancakes, complete with bacon? Or maybe a food truck that serves gourmet Mexican food or custom-made hot dogs? How about a six-foot-tall Jenga tower for entertainment? Or maybe a 40-foot rubber ducky as a backdrop?

## escort cards

Once you've narrowed down your reception theme within the "free spirit" genre, it's time to turn your attention to the details. (For example: how does one get a 40-foot rubber ducky to the reception site?) In the past few years, designers and about-to-be-married couples have been having a lot of fun with their reception decor, and that includes escort cards, place cards, menus, signage, banners, you name it — it's been a creative explosion.

Let's begin with escort cards, (a somewhat old-fashioned name). While not absolutely necessary at a wedding reception, they do let your guests know their table assignments, which is handy information if you'd like guests seated at specific tables. Escort cards can be simple, but they don't have to be boring. For example, if you're planning a 1980s-themed wedding, use pieces of neon-colored Washi Tape as name labels and place them on top of old cassette tapes.

Candies, especially chewy ones (like marshmallow Peeps), can serve as colorful and unexpected escort-card holders. Make cards by writing a guest's name onto a patterned piece of scrapbook paper; cut it into a flag-like shape. Attach it to a toothpick with hot glue; stick the toothpick in a Peep. Place the Peeps in alphabetical rows on your escort-card table.

For a school-themed wedding, you can make your own escort cards with lined loose-leaf paper, cut to fit onto prescored white tent cards. Write the guest's name in cursive, and include the table number (instead of "table," use "homeroom"). Or, encourage guests to do basic arithmetic (do the math, then find your table) by posting flash cards in which the answer to the problem reveals the table number.

If you want to make a display board, corkboard works well with small cards and quirky pins (which guests will love to take home).

Instead of a traditional card, give each guest a glass or bottle to take to his or her seat. Use a wineglass charm, a custom label, or tag to show each guest's name and table.

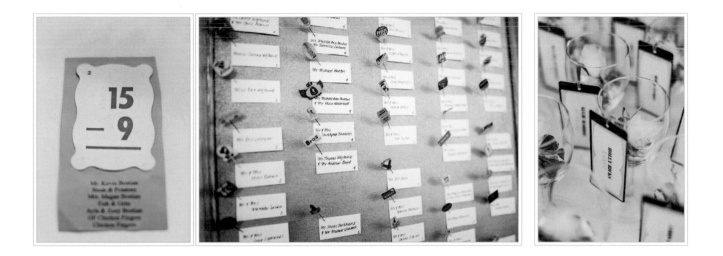

Rather than creating individual escort cards, you could provide instructions on a chalkboard sign, like this one, above left, which has a Beatles theme. Prefer no seating chart at all? Give guests a heads-up with a custom sign, inviting them to sit wherever they'd like.

Place cards, which are more formal, are not a requirement here. However, if you wish to personalize each guest's table setting, you can do so with a handwritten tent card, a custom tag around his or her water glass or wineglass, or a wrapped favor with a handwritten label.

## table numbers

Table numbers will help your guests find their seats quickly and easily. You can make your own quirky table numbers, using patterned fabric cut into a flag shape and hot glued around a wooden dowel. With a simple black marker, write the table number on it; place the flag in a mason jar or glass vase at the center of your table.

Prefer table names to numbers? Deck out your tables with signs in a specific theme, like the names of your favorite movies or singers. If you wish, include a short blurb about why the selected table name is significant to you.

Love is sweet
ERIKA & EMMANUEL
July 28, 2013

## guest book

A guest-book alternative can be created from "best wishes" or "advice" pages. Using your own computer, design and print out a stack of pages that provide a blank area for writing a guest's name, along with a smaller place to write best wishes or advice for

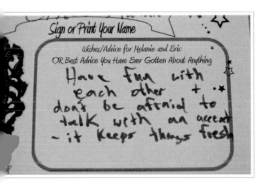

the couple. At your wedding, arrange a stack of the print-outs for guests to take, write on, and place in a basket; after the wedding, compile the sheets into a keepsake guest book chock-full of words of wisdom (and probably some funny quips).

To make a Jenga guest book, have guests write their well wishes on one side of a wooden block and sign their names on the reverse side. The blocks are then placed in a glass receptacle for the wedding couple to read later.

A printed book, particularly one that reflects your theme, can be used as a guest book. If your theme is dinosaurs, for instance, purchase a Dinosaur encyclopedia, and ask guests to flip through it and sign wherever they'd like.

If you'd like an artistic keepsake from your wedding, provide your guests with a large guest-book poster. This style of guest book uses inked thumbprints from guests, with a signature over the top of each thumbprint, to create a piece of art that the couple can frame after the wedding. For example, this print, above center, says "Love Is Sweet," and it includes a drawing of a cupcake. Guests added their thumbprints and signatures to make "sprinkles" on the cupcake.

## centerpieces

When designing your wedding centerpieces, don't be afraid to go wild. Traditional flowers are beautiful, but you should have a centerpiece, floral or not, that represents you as a couple. For instance, a stack of favorite books — *The Hobbit*, *The Hitchhiker's Guide to the Galaxy*, *The Lord of the Rings*, *The Empire Strikes Back*, or Sherlock Holmes titles, just to name a few — can be stacked or set upright to create a centerpiece. To incorporate a table number, use a paper clip to attach a numbered card to a page in the book.

For an added textural element, include a few paper flowers made from old books, either attached to stems and placed in a vase or set atop the books as decor. Need light? Place a battery-operated LED candle in a tea-light jar to add a romantic glow at nighttime.

Instead of using fresh flowers, create your own arrangements with whimsical floral picks, fabric floral blooms, and quirky banner flags. Place the items in a glass bottle, and display different arrangements at each table.

Another nonfloral idea is the pinwheel, which can be custom coordinated to tie into the rest of your decor. It gets bonus points, too, for being as whimsical as you can get.

One of my favorite centerpiece ideas is to use vintage records (or even handmade ones created to look like the real thing). This idea is perfect for a rockabilly or 1950s wedding, particularly for Beatles-enthused couples (and their guests). A small vase of flowers creates a focal point for the centerpiece and also acts as a prop for the records. If needed, you can stick the records together inconspicuously with clear tape, to ensure that they stand upright.

## entertainment

Dancing is a traditional favorite, but what about other reception activities (in addition to or instead of dancing)? For instance, if you and your spouse are having a game-themed wedding — or just happen to love playing Scrabble or Yahtzee on a regular basis — set up card tables with board games for guests to use. If you're planning an outdoor wedding, games like ladder golf, horseshoes, croquet, or corn toss will keep guests entertained for hours. A ping-pong tournament can also be a fun idea.

You can have a separate area for gamers to play, while other guests can boogie on the dance floor to your favorite tunes.

Instead of sit-down board games, some interactive indoor games can be fun for guests of all ages. Cat's cradle, one of my favorite string games, is an option that guests will remember from childhood (or learn all over again).

Supersized games, like a gigantic checker or chess board, lawn Scrabble (played with large cardboard signs with letters written on them), big playing cards, and oversized Jenga are a few entertainment choices to wow your guests.

While waiting for dinner, guests can sometimes get antsy (especially the younger ones). One of my favorite ideas for the table is to provide custom-created Mad Libs–style notepads related to your wedding. To make it even more fun, encourage guests to fill in the blanks "blindly," with the help of another guest. This results in a more hilarious story, worthy of your wedding scrapbook after the big day. You can use these pages in lieu of a traditional guest book, or solely for entertainment at tables.

Who says it's not appropriate to have a bounce house at a wedding? Sure, it wouldn't be the thing at a traditional wedding, but at an offbeat affair, it fits right in. Plus, who doesn't love a bounce house?

After dinner, have a projector and a big screen set up to play guests a favorite movie (*Star Wars*, anyone?). Serve popcorn and glass Coca-Cola bottles as a late-night snack, and lay out blankets for guests to sit and watch outdoors. Guests who love dancing can still stay indoors and dance the night away, while people who prefer a movie can relax and enjoy.

### PHOTO BOOTH

A photo booth is fun for guests of all ages, and, I might add, also provides some entertaining props for the dance floor. Let's face it: those boas, supersized glasses, and wigs aren't staying at the photo booth. To make yours a little more offbeat, use Polaroid cameras instead of a traditional booth; have guests snap photos and then display their antics using clothespins on a prestrung clothesline. Include a sign to let guests know what to do.

After the wedding, move the photos to your own wedding scrapbook to preserve the hilarious and heartfelt moments.

Need some prop ideas? For a literary theme, fill a jar with inexpensive, novelty eyeglass frames from a party-supply store. Guests can try them on and wear them all night. Or, have photo props attached to wooden dowels in the photo-booth area for guests to use

(and to return for others to borrow). For a geeky wedding, a set of necktie, mustache, and bow-tie props will fit right in.

Planning a superhero- or comic-book-themed wedding? Props that read "POW!" or "WHAM!" will make your photo booth even more memorable.

BOUQUET TOSS

The garter toss and bouquet toss, both of which happen at the reception, are traditional customs. Want to skip them? Go ahead. However, you could always incorporate your own unique twist instead. For instance, no one says that the bouquet toss *has* to be a bouquet. Get creative! At one reception, bride tossed a toy stuffed animal — a cat — to the crowd instead of a bouquet of flowers.

## favors

What will you give to guests as a sign of your sincere appreciation and thanks? One of my favorite ideas is a customized drink koozie, tied to your theme.

Temporary tattoos are fun for everyone to apply and wear. Look for quirky designs that reflects your theme, or consider ordering personalized versions.

Planning a *Star Wars*-themed wedding? Send guests home with a *Star Wars* soap trio, with R2-D2, Darth Vader, and a stormtrooper.

If you consider yourselves book nerds, send your guests home with handmade bookmarks or a miniature "book log" journal where guests can record books they're reading (or want to read in the future).

Want to give your guests something sweet? For a carnival- or circus-themed wedding, wrap boxes of animal crackers or Cracker Jacks or bags of circus-peanut candies for guests to enjoy.

Popcorn, cotton candy, and peanuts are other options which can be prepackaged in clear cellophane bags and personalized with your names and the wedding date. Or, popcorn can be served in carnival-inspired boxes, ready to eat (or to take).

Here's a sweetly creative idea: I once received a wedding invitation that requested we indicate on our response card whether we preferred superheroes, historians, or cartoons. I chose superheroes and at the reception I received a Wonder Woman Pez dispenser at my seat. It was fun to see guests' different Pez dispensers, which had been hand-selected for them by the bride and groom.

## food & drink

Serve guests your favorite food at your wedding, whether that means a BBQ buffet or an elegant, sit-down dinner with multiple courses. Is breakfast your favorite meal? Create a self-serve smorgasbord of cereal, juice, ice-cold milk (plus soy, almond, and lactose free), coffee, and cocktails. Or, try a top-your-own-pancakes bar: a chef prepares made-to-order pancakes in front of guests, using pancake batter and candies, chocolate chips, blueberries, bananas, or strawberries. Don't forget to include lots of bacon, sausage, eggs, and a fresh-fruit bar, too.

## the cake

Make your wedding cake a tad less traditional by adding a quirky cake topper. Plastic animal figurines — like dinosaurs — are sure to make your cake stand out. Customize them by adding a veil to the "bride" and a bowtie to the "groom." (See below, right).

A pair of custom cake toppers designed in your images is always a fun idea, especially because you can keep the toppers as mementos afterward. Charming animal toppers depicting the bride and groom is another option, especially if you are planning a wedding at a zoo (or just happen to love animals).

Instead of a cake topper, you can deck out your cake with thematic elements. For a steampunk wedding, consider a cake with edible "gear" embellishments and a slightly off-kilter pocket watch.

Surprise your groom with a special "groom's cake," designed with one of his favorite hobbies (like gaming) in mind.

Want to serve something sweet, but not a traditional cake? Opt for a unique treat, like doughnuts from your favorite bakery and ice-cold individual cartons of milk.

Or, create a giant cupcake that's the size of a wedding cake, topped with your photos held by fork tines.

## grand exit

When you make your grand exit, have guests say good-bye with a *Star Wars*-inspired lightsaber processional, or have guests wave whimsical pennant banners.

Making your grand exit outdoors at night? Opt for glow sticks instead!

The party doesn't have to end here. Explore the town with your photographer — maybe even stop by your favorite fast-food joint!

# Resources

page 179

M³ and Co. / www.etsy.com/shop/M3AndCo;
Little Woman Design / www.littlewomandesign.com
Ruff House Art / www.etsy.com/shop/ruffhouseart,
www.ruffhouseart.com

page 180

Crafty Pie Press / www.craftypie.com;
LetterBoxInk / www.etsy.com/shop/LetterBoxInk,
www.letterboxink.com;
Sparkvites / www.etsy.com/shop/Sparkvites,
http://sparkvites.com

page 183

Marbles Kids Museum / www.marbleskidsmuseum.org;
Museum of Life + Science / www.lifeandscience.org

page 188

Koyal Wholesale / www.koyalwholesale.com;
Betawife / www.etsy.com/shop/betawife

page 189

Etsy / www.etsy.com

page 190

Erica B Studios / www.etsy.com/shop/ericabstudios;
Kustom Kufflinks / www.kustomkufflinks.com

page 194

Zappos / www.zappos.com;
TOMS / www.toms.com

page 197

Converse / www.converse.com;
Dr. Martens / www.drmartens.com

page 199

When Geeks Wed / www.whengeekswed.com;
She Wore White / www.etsy.com/shop/sheworewhite;
Michelle's Clay Creations /
www.etsy.com/shop/MichellesClay

page 203

Washi Tape / www.cutetape.com/shop/japanese-
washi-masking-tape;
Peeps / www.peepsandcompany.com,
www.marshmallowpeeps.com

page 210

Pez / www.pez.com

# Traditional

If you're a bride-to-be who loves classic, time-tested wedding customs, this is the theme for you. In general, a "traditional" wedding adheres to conventional wedding practices. While this may be the most common theme, keep in mind that no two weddings are ever the same. Each bride and groom tell their own story and add their own personal touches to create a one-of-a-kind event. In this chapter, I'll share classic suggestions for your wedding day from beginning to end, along with fresh variations for modern couples.

# Invitations & More

As the first hint of what's to come, the invitations present an ideal opportunity to formally present your chosen theme to the guests. In this chapter, I'll show you examples of traditional and "modern" traditional invitations, as well as suggestions for wording.

## invitation suites

The traditional wedding invitation is still the most popular choice for engaged couples. It uses a classic typeface and is engraved on a heavy white or ecru-colored card stock, usually with a tissue overlay placed on top of the invitation. The bride's and groom's names appear in a script font, which is used to set their names apart from the rest of the text. Simple, clean borders, a hint of color in a frame or an envelope liner, and sometimes a motif are also typically found in a traditional invitation.

As many modern designers can attest to, traditional invitations don't have to be boring. Motifs like intertwined wedding bands and crosses, as well as fancy embossing, can all make an appearance in the design and still maintain a time-honored look. Consider using paper or card stock in black or with a shiny finish. Include ribbon, create a layout with a fold, or add a wrap to make a beautiful finishing touch.

The classic invitation suite includes: the invitation, an inner envelope, an outer envelope, a response card, a stamped and addressed response envelope, a reception card, and a map. Of course, there are always exceptions.

This lovely suite, above, from Jen Simpson Design, features some modern variations that are perfectly appropriate: the pale-pink frame, paired with a dramatic, slate-gray envelope; and a somewhat minimalist approach, with just the invitation, a response card, and printed directions to the ceremony site.

Shine Wedding Invitations, left, has taken a fresh approach to the traditional invitation by using a monogram in a classic font, along with a diagonal herringbone design, in mauve, for the envelope lining.

The reception card is most closely aligned with a traditional wedding; rarely do you see it elsewhere. At some traditional weddings, guests are invited to the ceremony only, and those who receive the reception card are invited to not only the ceremony, but also to a typically lavish affair just for family and close friends. Use the lower right corner of the reception card to note if there is a special dress code, such as black-tie attire. Never include registry information anywhere on the invitation.

Save-the-date cards are not required for this theme. However, if you'd like to give guests advance notice of your wedding date, you can send them a formal-photo card, using a photograph from your engagement session.

It is worth mentioning that when you send out formal wedding invitations, it is best to handwrite the names and the addresses of the invitees on the outer envelope. The inner envelope should include the handwritten names of the invitees, omitting the address.

### SUGGESTED WORDING

The hosts are mentioned first on the invitation. If the bride's parents are hosting, the invitation can begin with something like: "Mr. and Mrs. John Snow request the honor of your presence at the marriage of their daughter." (It is important to note that the phrase "the honor of your presence" traditionally means the ceremony will be held at a place of worship.) If both sets of parents are hosting together, the bride's parents are listed first, followed by the groom's parents. If the couple is hosting with both sets of parents, the invitation could read: "Together with their families, Miss Rebecca Smith and Mr. Douglas Snow request the honor of your presence. . . ."

If a parent is deceased, it is common to honor this parent by including his or her name on the invitation. This can be done with a simple reference, such as: "Miss Rebecca Smith, daughter of Samuel Smith and the late Jane Smith . . ."

# The Ceremony

The ceremony is the highlight of every wedding. In a traditional wedding, it is full of customs and practices that have endured through generations. In this section, I'll give you some ideas for a beautiful ceremony with a traditional tone, including a few contemporary alternatives.

## the venue

First, where will your ceremony be held? A traditional wedding is typically celebrated in a place of worship, such as a church, chapel, or synagogue.

While an indoor setting is not your only option, it does offer several advantages, like built-in seating, an existing backdrop — such as a chuppah or an altar — and a well-defined aisle.

Prefer an outdoor location? There are plenty of venues that can be adapted for a traditional wedding, such as a garden, a park, or a gazebo.

There's nothing like an outdoor wedding on a perfect summer's day. Since perfection can't be guaranteed, it's best to plan your outdoor traditional wedding with all possible weather conditions in mind, and that usually means renting an indoor space.

It's a pretty sure bet that if you're contemplating a ceremony and reception at a lake, in the mountains, at a public garden, or on a beach, there will be several nearby facilities to consider. Many venues will offer you a "menu" of options; packages include flowers (even the bouquet, boutonniere, and centerpieces) a rabbi, a minister, or an officiant; complete ceremony and reception setup, which includes tableware, food, service, and (nonalcoholic) beverages; photography; and a place for you to get ready. Sometimes, these packages are for a three- or four-hour period of time, so think about if that will work for you. Also, make your reservations early, especially at the more popular locations.

Even if you choose this "package" option, you can still put your personal stamp on a few things. Check with the facility to see if it's possible to add some handcrafted, personalized touches, such as signage, aisle and table decor, a focal point, escort cards, table numbers, and a guest-book area. Keep your additions practical, and remember that someone will have to clean it all up at the end.

## seating

For the seating of guests, follow proper (and traditional) wedding etiquette. At a formal church ceremony, the bride's family and friends are seated on the left, while the groom's are seated on the right. The first few rows are "reserved" for parents, other immediate family members, and special guests. For a traditional Jewish wedding, the bride's family and friends are seated on the right, while the groom's are seated on the left. During a Jewish ceremony, the parents of the bride and groom stand under the chuppah.

A church or synagogue provides convenient, ready-made seating for your guests, in the form of pew benches or chairs. If you are using an alternate ceremony space, you may need to rent your own seating. White folding chairs are the most basic and accessible solution. Another option is the Chiavari chair, which is available in many colors, including (but not limited to) white, black, and brown.

## aisle decor

Flower petals are the most popular and traditional choice for decorating your aisle, but not all churches or synagogues allow petals or an aisle runner. Be sure to check. The flower girl can sprinkle petals straight down the center, using white, pink, or red for a simple yet refined look. You can find artificial petals in these colors at craft stores like Michaels or Hobby Lobby, or online via Amazon. If you're outdoors and want an eco-friendly option, toss lavender or biodegradable confetti instead. You can find some beautiful options online at Flower Fetti.

If you prefer, an aisle runner can provide your decor instead. To add personalization, order a white aisle runner with your monogram on the end of it. Want to make your own? Buy a cotton/polyester blend fabric, and cut it to fit the width and length of your aisle. Use large monogram stencils, a brush, and ink to apply your monogram. For staying power, cover it with a clear coat of acrylic spray paint. Depending on the floor surface, you may need a nonslip mat underneath.

An elegant floral arrangement can be placed in a moss or burlap pew cone, tied to a ribbon, and used to decorate the entire aisle (or a special reserved section). Check out the Etsy store Burlap Pew Cones for beautiful holders and baskets.

One of my favorite twists on aisle decor is to use photographs of the couple from childhood. Hang framed photos along the edge of the aisle, with one on every other chair or pew bench.

Your altar can be decorated with clear glass vases full of flowers. After the ceremony, transport them to the reception for added decor.

For an outdoor ceremony, use moderation when decorating your ceremony space. If the setting is already beautiful — lush gardens, green grass, and a pebble-lined walkway, for instance — accentuate the natural scenery by keeping the aisle decor minimal. A simple ribbon bow is all it takes to transform a white folding chair into one that's elegant enough for an aisle.

A dramatic arch can be added to an outdoor location as a ceremony focal point. Create your own arch with full, natural-toned floral blooms (like hydrangeas or roses), and incorporate plenty of greenery for lushness and visual impact.

A gazebo, either at a favorite park or a wedding or event venue, provides a classic ceremony spot and a backdrop that's perfect for photographs.

## ceremony programs

While not a requirement, a ceremony program is a formality that is most commonly found at traditional weddings.

A traditional wedding program is typically presented in booklet form, and it should coordinate with your wedding invitations. The program will feature your names on the front, along with the wedding date. Inside the booklet, list the names of the members of the wedding party, as well as the names of both sets of parents. The order of the proceedings in the ceremony should be included, with notations on special traditions or readings (plus the readers' names). Music and readings should also be listed in the program.

A thank-you message can be included in the program, letting your guests know how much you appreciate them for taking part in your wedding ceremony.

For ceremony programs, menus, and more, try Beacon Lane or Lama Works, two fantastic options.

## traditions

For a traditional wedding, it's especially important to include long-standing customs, since they define your theme. (Of course, it is your wedding, and you can choose to do anything you'd like.) Here are a few wedding traditions to consider for your ceremony.

### ESCORTING THE BRIDE

The father walking his daughter down the aisle is a long-held tradition. Way back in the day, it was the culmination of an agreement, usually a financial one, between two families to join a son and a daughter. The daughter was the property of her father, so this tradition literally symbolizes his "giving her away" to a new family.

Today, having your father (or any other important person in your life) accompany you down the wedding aisle is a memorable moment. If your dad isn't available for any reason, it's absolutely okay to ask your mom, your groom's dad, or a friend to accompany you — or even to walk it solo.

### SOMETHING OLD, SOMETHING NEW . . .

"Something old, something new, something borrowed, something blue, and a silver sixpence in your shoe" is a traditional formula for wedding attire that modern-day brides still like to follow. To have all of the above is believed to bring good luck to the bride, but whether or not that's true is anyone's guess. (It's fun to do, regardless!)

These items are easier to acquire than you may think. For instance, something old can be a special handkerchief from your mother that you can wrap around the handle of your bouquet. Something new is, in most cases, the dress. For something borrowed, ask for a piece of jewelry from your grandmother — perhaps a brooch clipped onto your clutch. My favorite something-blue trend is a pair of blue heels, which you'll enjoy wearing during the wedding and beyond.

Or, you could choose a pair of topaz earrings (treated with heat to bring out the blue), a dress tag embroidered with blue thread, a garter with a blue ribbon, or a blue hairpin.

A quaint something-blue tradition is to have your bridesmaids sign their names on the soles of your shoes, using a blue permanent marker. (At the end of the night, the woman with the name that is still legible is considered the next to marry.)

## CEREMONY MUSIC

Like many aspects of a traditional wedding, there are customs and time-honored conventions when it comes to the music. Basically, there's entrance music and exit music, and it varies depending on who is entering or exiting.

Welcome music begins about half an hour before the ceremony, as the guests enter. It changes when the family walks to their seats, and again when the wedding party enters. (The changes in the music cue the guests that something different is about to happen, or that different groups are making their way down the aisle.) The big show-stopper is, of course, when the bride appears, and her music is completely different from everyone else's.

When selecting your processional music, consider a traditional piece, like "Here Comes the Bride" (the common name for Wagner's "Bridal Chorus"), or Pachelbel's "Canon in D." For a Jewish ceremony, "Ani L'Dodi V'Dodi Li" is a customary choice.

## RECESSIONAL

In a traditional church ceremony, the bride and groom walk down the aisle after being proclaimed husband and wife, after which they sign the marriage certificate.

For a traditional Jewish ceremony, the couple concludes the ceremony with the "breaking of the glass," after which the bride and groom go down the aisle and sign the ketubah.

For a military wedding, the bride and groom proceed down the aisle under a traditional arch of sabers.

# ring bearer & flower girl

The ring bearer's role in a traditional wedding is to carry the couple's rings in a vessel to the altar, where the best man holds the rings until it's time to exchange vows. It is customary for the ring bearer to carry a decorative ring pillow, with the rings attached to the top with a ribbon. The ring pillow should coordinate with the overall decor and color palette of the wedding.

For a contemporary alternative, use a "ring bag" instead. A ring bag is a drawstring muslin bag, hand stamped with your initials and the wedding date on the front.

The flower girl's role at a traditional wedding is simple: to toss petals! If she is old enough to handle the task, give her a traditional flower basket to carry (usually covered in satin, and embellished with flowers or ribbons). In the spring and summer months, a moss-covered basket can be used instead.

Fill the basket with white, pink, or red petals. Have her proceed down the aisle before you, so that your path will be covered with petals prior to your grand entrance. If the flower girl is too young to scatter petals, have her hold a small flower bouquet or a flower ball with a ribbon for carrying. You can make your own flower ball by hot gluing faux flowers to a Styrofoam ball and attaching a looped ribbon as a handle.

# wedding-party gifts

It is customary for the bride and groom to give a gift to members of their wedding party, including the bridesmaids, groomsmen, flower girl, and ring bearer. The gift does not need to be extravagant; rather, it should be a token of your appreciation. It is also important to note that gifts should not be the same for each recipient, but instead tailored to his or her unique tastes. To make the gesture more meaningful, include a handwritten note or card with each gift. Here are a few ideas to get you started.

## BRIDESMAIDS

For bridesmaids, a traditional gift is a clutch purse — take a look at Angee W. on Etsy, who has some fantastic designs — a pair of earrings, or a necklace. For a special touch, consider adding a custom detail: a personalized tag stitched into the inside of her clutch, a pair of earrings that feature her birthstone, or a necklace with a monogram charm using the first letter of her name. As an added keepsake gift, customize the wooden hangers for your gown and your bridesmaids' dresses. I like the work at Get Hung Up on Etsy. For a DIY version, use a permanent wood marker to personalize each hanger with the attendant's name and title (either "Maid of Honor" or "Bridesmaid").

Gifts don't have to be overly complicated; a framed photo of you and your bridesmaid together makes a nice memento. For a gift she'll use, treat her to a spa or salon gift certificate to get her hair and nails done, or get her a gift card from her favorite store so she can spoil herself after the wedding.

### GROOMSMEN

For a traditional groomsmen gift, consider collar stays, a flask, a watch, a tie bar, or a pair of cuff links. Personalization — such as engraving his initials on a flask or buying a pair of cuff links with the logo of his favorite sports team — will make the gift more meaningful. Surprise the best man with a set of cuff links featuring his initials. One handmade source is White Truffle studio. If you're considering a flask or etched glassware — like custom pilsner glasses — a source I like is The Wedding Gallery by Brad Goodell. For collar stays and tie bars, try Spiffing Jewelry. A cigar humidor, a bottle of his favorite liquor, or tickets to a sporting event or concert are other gift ideas to consider. I've heard of a groom giving each of his groomsmen a portable BBQ grill and a custom sports-team cover. I like this idea because it is both personal and functional. When you're picking out the gift, consider something that suits him and that you know he'll enjoy.

### FLOWER GIRL & RING BEARER

For the flower girl, a piece of jewelry made just for her or a small purse is an ideal choice. Consider giving your ring bearer a "ring-bearer badge" that he can wear instead of a boutonniere (I love the ones at Knotty Notions on Etsy). For both the ring bearer and the flower girl, a toy given to them after the ceremony is a great way to show your appreciation.

## transportation

For a traditional wedding, the bride typically travels to the ceremony with her parents, and the groom is transported by the best man. After the ceremony, the wedding party usually travels together to the reception, either in a limousine or a limo bus that the newlyweds have arranged and paid for. If you prefer, the wedding party can drive separately, and the bride and groom can travel together in their own car. However, I recommend traveling as one group; that way, you can stop to take photographs and share a few special Champagne toasts. Plus, hiring a driver eliminates the stress of driving yourselves, so you can relax, unwind, and get excited for the party that's about to take place at your reception.

If you're planning a classic wedding, consider transportation that has an elegant, old-fashioned feel, like a vintage Rolls-Royce.

# The Attire

Now that you have some ideas for your ceremony, it's time to think about what you — and your entire wedding party — will wear to it. Let's start with some traditional bridal-attire options for you to consider.

## the bride

Earlier in this chapter, I mentioned a few traditions that take place during the ceremony. Tradition also plays a big role in wedding attire, with the bride's dress at the top of the list, followed by the veil. Most notably, the traditional bride should wear a white dress as a symbol of purity. In more modern weddings, ivory or champagne can be worn. The gown is customarily floor length, and it includes a short or long train. A classic bridal gown is made of silk, taffeta, or lace, with or without sleeves.

While these conventions are the norm for a traditional wedding, I recommend that each bride selects the dress she loves the most, rather than basing her selection on established "rules." You'll only be wearing the dress once, so you ought to absolutely love it.

Another customary piece of attire is the bridal veil, whether it is elbow length, fingertip, or cathedral length, just to name a few options. While it is unlikely that no one else will wear a white dress to the ceremony, it is certain that only the bride will be wearing a veil.

In keeping with tradition, pearls are a bride's staple. Whether you wear a strand of pearls, borrow a pair of pearl earrings from your mother, or wear a modern pearl pendant, you'll want to incorporate this jewelry custom into your wedding-day ensemble.

White or ivory pumps are another classic style for the bride (although, as with all wedding decisions, your shoe selection is completely up to you).

With a traditional wedding, the bride and groom usually don't see each other before the nuptials. If you prefer to follow this custom, consider sending him a gift or a handwritten note before you walk down the aisle. It's a sweet way to convey your sentiments before the ceremony, while still remaining unseen.

Likewise, he may send you a note or a gift while you're getting ready. My recommendation: wait until the very last moment to apply mascara, and be certain that it is waterproof.

It is also customary for the bride to get ready with her bridesmaids on the morning of the wedding. For a personalized touch, everyone can wear a monogrammed robe or shirt (which will look great in those coveted "getting ready" photos).

Finally, it is tradition for the bride's mother to put on her veil — the finishing touch before the bride enters the ceremony.

## bridesmaids

For a traditional wedding, bridesmaids either wear dresses in a neutral tone — like pale yellow, taupe, or beige — or they coordinate their outfits with the wedding's color palette.

Did you know that in decades past, the bride would deliberately select a bridesmaid dress that was unflattering on her "maids," so that the bride would look the best at the wedding? Thankfully, today's brides are friendlier to the members of their wedding party.

Since your bridesmaids will do so much to support you on your special day, be sure to choose dresses that you know they'll love. Traditionally, the bridesmaid dresses should complement each other and be similar in style. Also, keep in mind your bridesmaids' comfort level: pick a shorter dress in the warmer months and a longer dress (in a heavier, warmer fabric) for fall and winter weddings.

Another classic option for bridesmaids is a black dress; it's always in style, and it coordinates nicely with the groomsmen's tuxedos.

## groom & groomsmen

For the groom and groomsmen, a tuxedo is the time-honored choice. Pair a black tuxedo with a dress shirt, a black bow tie or necktie, and a pocket square.

Groomsmen should always wear coordinating attire to match the groom. If you want the groom to look more distinct, he can wear a vest or a different-colored tie.

Another favorite groomsmen look is a tailored suit in gray, black, or beige. Complete the ensemble with a dress shirt, a neutral tie, a pocket square, and a coordinating boutonniere.

It's common for the bridesmaid dresses and groomsmen's ties to coordinate in color. For instance, if the bridesmaids are wearing blue, the tie and vest should correspond. Similarly, the boutonnieres should relate to the bridesmaids' bouquets, either by using the same type of flowers or by wrapping the stems of the boutonnieres and bouquets in a matching ribbon color.

For footwear, the groom and groomsmen typically wear black or brown dress shoes, depending on what works with their attire.

## ring bearer & flower girl

The ring bearer's attire should closely reflect that of the groom and groomsmen. If they are wearing a suit, then he should, too. However, the suit doesn't have to be in the same color.

For traditional weddings, the flower girl's dress is typically white to complement the bride's. The flower girl doesn't have to adorn her hair, but she'd feel like a real princess in a wreath or crown made of baby's breath, a floral headband, or a tiara.

Shoes can be neutral in color and should be comfortable for both of them to wear down the aisle.

# The Flowers

When it comes to flowers for your traditional wedding ceremony, conventional blooms are usually the best option. In this section, I'll share a few of my favorite recommendations for flowers to include in the bouquets and boutonnieres.

## the bouquet

White tulips make a lovely bridal bouquet and don't require any additional "fillers," but you can add spots of color with a bouquet wrap. Tulips are in season in late spring.

Another traditional choice is the hydrangea, particularly in white. Since these blooms are naturally large in size, you only need a handful to create a breathtaking bridal bouquet.

Stephanotis — a flower known for its signature, trumpet-shaped blossom — is used as an accent with other blooms, such as roses. Stephanotis has a remarkable fragrance and is available year-round. (I had roses paired with stephanotis in my own bridal bouquet, and I can still recall its wonderful scent.)

Other flowers to consider include daisies, sunflowers, roses, anemones, freesia, irises, peonies, lilacs, and calla lilies, just to name a few.

Baby's breath is a surprisingly elegant option for bridesmaid bouquets. It is so affordable that you can create an extremely full bouquet for a fraction of the cost of a more typical bouquet. Baby's breath is becoming increasingly popular because of its beauty, though, not its price.

## boutonnieres

As with all wedding themes, the boutonnieres worn by the groom and groomsmen should be selected after the bouquets, so that they will coordinate. If you're opting for an understated bridal bouquet — using white roses, for instance — have a boutonniere created for the groom that mimics the look and feel of your bouquet.

A calla-lily stem is one of my favorite traditional boutonniere options. A single calla lily is so dramatic that it hardly needs further embellishments.

### CORSAGES

It is customary to honor the special women in your life — the bride's mom, the groom's mom, and grandmothers — by giving each of them a corsage to wear at the wedding. Coordinate the flowers in the corsage with those in your bouquet.

# The Reception

One of the biggest parties of your life will be your wedding reception. In this section, I'll show you the best traditional-themed ideas for choosing your venue, decor, favors, entertainment, cake, and more.

## the venue

Some of the most classic venues for a traditional wedding reception are a tented outdoor area, a banquet hall, and an elegant ballroom.

Specialty hotels or banquet-hall facilities are designed for events like weddings, so you know that they will have tables, chairs, and catering services available. Plus, since these venues work with wedding couples on a regular basis, their staffs will be prepared to accommodate your theme, your wedding size, and your meal preferences.

Before you decide on a specific venue, it's important that you conduct adequate research. If you're considering a local facility, make sure that you visit all of the contenders. This will give you an opportunity to meet with the staff and tour the grounds of each one. If the location will be out of state, see if the facility has a Web site with a photo gallery. Also, look online for reviews from couples that have had their own weddings there, so that you can get a clear picture of how yours would look and how well the venue would handle your event. Before you commit, be sure to speak to a manager on the phone and go over any questions you may have.

## OUTDOOR VENUES

If you have space, and if the weather permits, consider a tented reception. You can create your own dream venue — it will have all the comforts of an indoor space, plus the added beauty and charm of an outdoor setting (while still offering shelter from wind or rain, if needed).

If you're designing the decor yourself, add a few strands of twinkle lights. Rent tables and chairs, and provide linens and centerpieces.

For a more formal effect, hang a chandelier, rent white tables and chairs, and use white linens in your decor.

## cocktail hour

A cocktail hour takes place before the wedding dinner is served. You should use formal glassware (as opposed to plastic) and bar accessories, like serving trays, gold-rimmed glassware, and cocktail napkins.

For a traditional wedding, the bride and groom may suggest a signature cocktail for guests, or the regular house favorites can be served; beer, wine, and liquor are time-tested celebratory drinks. A Champagne toast typically takes place once the wedding toasts begin.

## escort cards

When guests arrive at your reception, they'll want to know where to be seated. Traditionally, escort cards are used to inform guests of their table assignments, and to make them feel both invited and welcomed. Since a traditional wedding is more formal, escort cards are strongly encouraged. Ask your invitation designer if he or she can create them. Set up an escort-card table near the reception entrance. Write each guest's name and table assignment on a folded tent card, and arrange them in alphabetical order.

Or, you can display lists of table assignments, instead of using individual tent cards. For example, if you have selected a wine motif for your traditional wedding, you could use wine corks to create a corkboard, and then pin the table assignments onto it.

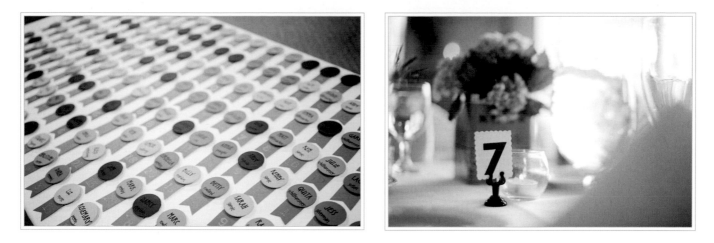

## TABLE NUMBERS

Clear, easy-to-read table numbers will help each guest find his or her assigned table. If you've chosen a low-profile centerpiece, follow suit with a simple, low-profile table number. You can make table numbers from your computer and printer, using plain black numerals and scalloped paper cutouts. Insert each table number into a simple black or white card holder (available at craft stores).

Even in a traditional wedding, table names can be a fun, permissible alternative to the usual numbers. Consider using a few names that reflect you as a couple, whether they are places you visited during your courtship, places on the map where wedding guests are originally from, or places you plan to go on your honeymoon. The extra personalization is a great conversation starter for your guests.

## PLACE CARDS

If you've decided to make specific table assignments, be sure to include a place card at each guest's seat. Displaying a handwritten tent card is the simplest and most appropriate way to welcome each guest to his or her seat. Plus, it's easy to find white tent cards at your local craft store, and personalizing them isn't a very time-consuming task.

## guest book

For a traditional wedding, it is customary for guests to sign an actual book. Typically, a traditional guest book is covered in satin or silk, and has lined interior pages for guests to leave their names and well wishes. I've often been asked why a couple needs a guest book at all — is it really necessary? When planning my own wedding a few years ago, I also wondered if a guest book was a requirement, but now I'm very glad I had one. I still enjoy looking back on the messages from guests, including a few loved ones who have since passed — I am so happy to have had them present at my wedding.

If you prefer a more contemporary version of a guest book, you can make your own heart-shaped paper cutouts on which guests can write their names and personal messages. Place the paper hearts in a decorative vase or bowl, along with a small container of pens and a framed set of instructions. After the wedding, the personalized hearts can be arranged into a work of art that can be framed.

## table decor

This wedding theme calls for elegant dinner plates, formal silverware, and linen napkins. For a refined touch, you can accent your napkins with rings. Make your own napkin rings by wrapping a thin piece of fabric around the napkin and securing it with a twine-and-bead closure.

Traditional wedding centerpieces typically involve floral displays in vases, along with romantic candlelight. One particularly beautiful style is a "submerged" centerpiece, in which a flower is submerged underwater within a clear, narrow glass vase. If you'd like, you can add a floating candle to finish the look and provide light for the tabletop.

Low-profile floral arrangements, placed in decorative vases, are both attractive and practical. The modest height of these centerpieces ensures that guests can share in conversation across the table. Also, you can make them yourself; simply fill decorative glassware in varying heights with a single stem, such as a rose or dahlia.

For a dramatic statement, create centerpieces with bright, colorful blooms (see photograph on page 246). For this type of centerpiece, place the flowers in an "Eiffel Tower" vase, which is extra tall in size. Find them in assorted sizes online at Save on Crafts. Use a clear vase, so that guests on opposite sides of the table can still see each other. Enhance the centerpiece with short, square candleholders or bud vases with neutral blooms.

## THE HEAD TABLE

At a traditional wedding, the bride and groom sit with the wedding party at a "head table," usually placed in the center of the room against a wall, facing the dance floor. This scenario allows the bride and groom to be front and center for toasts and photos, and makes it easy for guests to mingle with them before dinner.

## customs

I'm sure you're familiar with some of the most common reception customs, such as the garter removal and toss, the bouquet toss, and wedding toasts. While they are completely optional, it can be very entertaining to include these time-tested traditions in your own reception.

For tossing the garter, your groom may find it more fun to throw (and more fun for guests to catch) when it is combined with a sports element. Simply wrap the garter around a miniature football or basketball prior to tossing.

Another notable tradition is the bouquet toss, in which the bride throws her bouquet (or a special tossing bouquet) to the single female guests. Tradition states that the woman who catches the bouquet will be the next to marry.

The offering of wedding toasts, which happens before dinner is served, is another notable tradition. The emcee will introduce the maid (or matron) of honor, who will offer the first toast, followed by the best man.

## wedding favors

It is customary for the couple to give their guests a token of appreciation in the form of a wedding favor. A long-established tradition is to give guests a symbolic number of white Jordan almonds, placed in a favor bag. There should be five Jordan almonds for each guest: one for health, one for wealth, one for happiness, one for fertility, and one for longevity.

Giving guests sweets to take home (or to enjoy at the reception) is another favor option. One of my favorites is a home-baked cookie, like a wedding-embellished sugar cookie with your initials written in icing.

I also love the idea of a wedding bell at each guest's seat as a wedding favor. Guests can ring the bell to get the couple to kiss (rather than clanking on glassware). A bell is an especially nice touch for a winter wedding.

## entertainment

A traditional wedding isn't complete without music — whether live or played by a deejay — and plenty of dancing! For this wedding theme, you'll want to include the traditional dances, beginning with the "first dance" as newlyweds.

This dance is followed by the sweet and tearful dance between the bride and the father of the bride, and then the groom and the mother of the groom will share a dance. To make these traditions even sweeter, reach out and ask what songs he and she would like to select for their special dances. These will soon become favorite tunes, just like "That's What Friends Are For" by Dionne Warwick and Friends is now one of mine. Plus, the bride's father and the groom's mother will feel comfortable dancing to the chosen song, since they are already familiar with its tempo and lyrics.

Another tradition is the "wedding-party dance," in which the bride and groom share a song with the groomsmen and bridesmaids. For this dance, the best man and maid (or matron) of honor share a dance together (and the remaining groomsmen and bridesmaids are paired up however you choose). Select a song that is meaningful to you (and to the group). If you'd prefer a faster dance (or even a choreographed one, which can be quite amusing for your guests), choose a song you know they'll love.

A joyous part of a Jewish wedding reception is the *hora*, or chair dance, set to the tune of "Hava Nagila."

Additional dances are up to you, but they are highly recommended to keep guests entertained. For instance, a conga line is optional . . . although my family would insist that it is a requirement.

## MUSIC

When you're selecting music with your deejay (or wedding band), include some crowd-pleasers to ensure that guests will be eager to dance. "We Are Family" and "Y.M.C.A." are tunes that are typically played at weddings, since all guests know them and aren't afraid to dance along. If there are songs that make you cringe, put them on a "do not play" list. And, finally, let guests make special requests to the emcee, using request forms that you have provided at the reception tables or at the deejay's booth. When guests hear "their song," they're more likely to get up and dance — and to bring others along.

## CIGAR BAR

Weddings are among the occasions that people have historically celebrated with cigars. If you'd like to offer your guests this option, provide a box of favorite cigars, matches, an outdoor area, and a receptacle to extinguish the cigars properly. You can make your own receptacle, using a galvanized pail filled with sand.

## the cake

According to tradition, the wedding cake usually contains two, three, or more tiers. The most traditional wedding cake is cherry nut; however, contemporary couples often select their favorite flavor and filling instead.

The cutting of the cake is a custom that takes place at the beginning of the reception, when the bride and groom cut the first slice of cake and serve it to each other.

The first slice is cut from the top tier, which is then wrapped and frozen for one year, so that it can be eaten on the couple's first wedding anniversary.

For any wedding theme, using custom cake toppers is one of the easiest ways to personalize your cake. There are some classic-with-a-twist toppers online at The Pink Owl Designs or Lynn's Little Creations. Consider ordering cake toppers that resemble you as a couple.

In addition to cake, coffee should be served to guests following dinner. You can also set up a dessert bar, where guests can choose tempting sweets to enjoy with their coffee.

## grand exit

Once you're ready to leave the reception at the end of the night, make it a grand exit. Give guests packets of confetti to toss, and have plenty of photographs taken to capture the moment. Here is a strong hint to pass along to the members of the wedding party: decorating the getaway car with a "Just Married" decal or with tin cans tied to string is a fun way to surprise the bride and groom as they embark on their honeymoon.

# Resources

Page 219

Jen Simpson Design / www.jensimpsondesign.com,
www.etsy.com/shop/jensimpsondesign;
Shine Wedding Invitations /
www.shineweddinginvitations.com,
www.etsy.com/people/shineinvitations

Page 223

Chiavari / www.bestchiavarichairs.com

Page 224

Michaels Stores / www.michaels.com;
Hobby Lobby / www.hobbylobby.com;
Amazon / www.amazon.com;
Flower Fetti / www.etsy.com/shop/flowerfetti;
Burlap Pew Cones /
www.etsy.com/shop/burlappewcones

Page 225

Beacon Lane / www.etsy.com/shop/beaconlane;
Lama Works / www.etsy.com/shop/lamaworks

Page 230

Angee W. / www.etsy.com/shop/angeew;
Get Hung Up / www.etsy.com/shop/gethungup

Page 231

White Truffle / www.whitetrufflestudio.com;
The Wedding Gallery by Brad Goodell /
www.etsy.com/shop/bradgoodell;
Spiffing Jewelry / www.etsy.com/shop/spiffingjewelry;
Knotty Notions / www.etsy.com/shop/knottynotions

Page 245

Save-on-Crafts / www.save-on-crafts.com

Page 250

The Pink Owl Designs / www.etsy.com/shop/
thepinkowldesigns;
Lynn's Little Creations / www.etsy.com/shop/
lynnslittlecreations

# Boho Style

If your idea of a perfect wedding combines traditional elements with a modern bohemian flair, then a boho-style celebration may be right up your alley. What is boho style? It's a relaxed aesthetic, pleasantly reminiscent of an era when one wore head scarves, gauzy dresses, and loose hairstyles. It's a touch of floral and a pinch of ethnic, with a romantic hippie influence. Creativity and nature are celebrated in all aspects of boho style.

# Invitations & More

In keeping with the relaxed attitude of the boho theme, you can have a lot of fun with your invitations — there are no rules! However, to ensure that all of the elements of your wedding are cohesive, setting the tone from the beginning is essential. Save-the-date cards will give your guests a hint of what to expect on your wedding day. If you are planning a destination wedding, be sure to mail the save the dates a few months earlier than the invitations.

## invitation suites

A boho-style wedding is brimming with contrasts. For the invitations, this may mean pairing typographic flourishes with a muted palette. On the other hand, it's not unusual for designers to use colors like bright turquoise — inspired by tiles from Morocco, the modern-day land of the bohemians.

A modern boho tone can be established through the creative use of motifs, like the vintage flower patterns in this suite, above, from Blue Magpie Invitations. Other motifs include feathers, antique ribbons, and lace. When you find a design that you love, keep in mind that you can also order coordinating items, such as wedding-favor tags, ceremony programs, escort cards, and table numbers.

I absolutely love how the designers at Hoopla Love, below right, have created a fun, carefree vibe by using retro-style photos and a charming, hand-drawn map.

Below left, Jen Simpson Design has created a stunning suite that combines cursive lettering in muted, oceanic tones with a chevron-patterned envelope lining.

# The Ceremony

There are special places that evoke the ambience of specific wedding themes. For a boho-inspired celebration, a warm summer's day spent in nature would strike the perfect note. But if an outdoor wedding is not possible, you can always decorate your indoor space to create the mood you're looking for.

## the venue

Where is the perfect spot for you to tie the knot? A waterfront site, a rose garden, a cottage, or maybe a historic manor house? The deciding factors should be that the location is romantic, that it suits you and your sweetheart's personal style, and that it inspires both of you. Once you've found the ideal setting, make it your own with customized accents and ceremonial elements.

## aisle decor

Create a ceremony aisle that is worthy of your big day. Since ceremonies can be held almost anywhere, I've got plenty of ideas for both indoor and outdoor affairs.

I love the paper cones filled with tall ferns in the photograph on the opposite page. The aisle decor is simple, yet the ferns bring height, movement, and texture to the area. Smaller versions of these kind of arrangements can also be hung from the backs of the chairs (although not every chair needs to be decorated).

Here are some ideas that can be used inside or out: For an evening ceremony, add subtle lighting by placing small groupings of LED votives or a large white lantern from IKEA at the end of each row. Use round, medium-size kissing balls or pom-poms made of fresh flowers, folded paper, or even pinecones; attach twine or strips of fabric to the balls, and then hang them from the chairs or even tree branches. Lengths of satin ribbon or cording can be tied in big, beautiful bows to each chair, or use bright, oversized paper flowers instead — they will be especially vivid when paired with an eye-catching aisle runner. Speaking of aisle runners, you'll find a world of offerings on handmade-craft sites like Etsy: striped, chevron, solid, burlap, woven grass, monogrammed, and printed with your motif.

To frame the area where you will be exchanging your vows, consider creating a backdrop or focal point. Outside locations can feature an arch like the one below right, which has a distinctly boho feel. The arch, below left, has been decorated with a length of light, transparent fabric and some flowers; both are relatively simple to assemble and style.

For an indoor venue, a fabric backdrop can be stretched between poles or hung from a pipe. The range of material to use is endless. If you go for the hanging effect, just make sure that the fabric drapes well. Create layers by overlapping pieces and adding a swag or two. Another indoor idea to consider is placing large potted plants on either side of the ceremony area — they will help to define the space. String some miniature white lights in and around the greenery, and finish off the look with a small rug to stand on.

## ring bearer & flower girl

Instead of using a traditional ring pillow, the ring bearer could carry a decorative box. Buy a small wooden one from a craft store, and give it a weathered look by applying a special, white paint treatment. You can buy a kit (in a "distressed ivory" color) by Rust-Oleum, which makes ordinary wood look more worn. Line the box with a piece of velvet and place the rings inside the box for him to carry down the aisle.

The flower girl could toss traditional rose petals, but have you thought of lavender flowers instead? As they are stepped on, the scent is heavenly. Flower-girl baskets made of moss — lined with plastic or with an insert — are relatively new additions to wedding decor. You can find them online from Etsy shops such as Teresa's Plants & More or Superior Craft Supply.

## transportation

Getting from one place to another on your wedding day can mean many things. Maybe you're having family members or friends meet out-of-town guests at their hotel, then escort them to the ceremony and reception site. If that's the case, consider hiring a classic limo or a couple of antique cars, complete with drivers. Guests will arrive at your wedding in style. If you're getting married on an island, and will have to rent a private boat to ferry guests to and from the mainland, bring some pashmina wraps in case it's chilly — they will appreciate it.

For your entrance (and exit), consider a vintage coupe or horse-drawn carriage. Either would be a perfect backdrop for pre- and post-ceremony photographs.

# The Attire

There are three things to keep in mind while shopping for your wedding gown, regardless of your theme: it has to fit, it has to flatter, and it has to make you feel fantastic. It's one of the most important days of your life, and your attire should make you smile from ear to ear. Don't compromise — keep looking until you find the right dress.

## the bride

If you are a bohemian at heart and are thinking of wearing a boho-style wedding gown, you'll have many options to consider. Some contemporary designers are turning their attention to the styles of the 1960s "hippie" era, because they offer such creative freedom. Whether you decide on an existing design, a vintage dress or a customized

piece, your gown should always reflect your personality and the occasion. If you love boho style, you'll want to incorporate vintage textiles, lace and trim, taffeta, and layers of beautiful, hand-dyed and pleated silks to create a romantic, feminine silhouette. Adornments such as beading, crystals, embroidery, appliques, and fringe are a must-have details to add to the gown, the headpiece, the shoes, and even the hair ornament.

Lengths can be to the floor and flowing, mid-calf, or short. Pants are not out of the question, especially if they are long and billowy. Accessories like jewelry have their own boho-style category, making it easy to find necklaces, earrings, and bracelets in secondhand stores or online.

Footwear can be anything from gladiator sandals to white thigh-high boots to beaded ballet slippers. And don't discount five-inch heels with special details, like straps, buckles, fringes, tassels, sequins, or studs.

There are several boho-style options for adorning your hair. Skip the veil and don a halo of greenery and blooms for the ultimate in bohoness. Or wear a flower in your hair. This simple net veil, above right, makes a statement when accented with an oversized silk flower. For lovely, handcrafted halos, hand-beaded headbands, and floral crowns, check out Mignonne Handmade online.

Headscarves are definitely part of the boho wardrobe. I can easily see how a vintage fingertip veil or length of fine lace would make a stunning headscarf or knotted head wrap.

If you'd like to wear a veil, how about one you can add your own handcrafted touches to? Some ideas include adding a silk flower or a jeweled fascinator; a decorative edging of lace, fabric, or tiny beads; embroidery or applique.

## bridesmaids

I'll bet that when you ask friends or family members to be bridesmaids at your upcoming boho-style wedding, the response will be an emphatic "Yes!" They know it will be a fun and slightly unconventional event, and that they'll probably get a dress they can wear again. Share with them your color palette, some texture ideas, and a price range. If you have a suggestion for places to shop, like J. Crew or online at Free People, let them know. Likewise, check out Etsy for some lovely dresses from shops such as Aya Bridal or Atelier Signature. The dresses are custom made to the measurements you provide, and some shops offer a discount if you order several dresses at a time.

All styles are up for grabs: a maxi dress, knee length, or a mini; short sleeves or sleeveless; A-line or Empire; a slip dress or a halter — anything goes. If the party will extend into the evening hours, consider a cover-up: a pashmina, cardigan, bolero, or shrug. Their hairstyles shouldn't veer too far from your style, but if you decide to wear something in your hair, you could have something similar made for each of them. Their footwear will also take a lead from yours.

## groom & groomsmen

I'm not sure that men get as excited about boho-style as women do, but if he is game to participate, he won't regret it. At the very least, he'll appreciate the fact that your big day won't be as formal as a traditional wedding, even if he's not inclined to go all out. A lightweight linen suit that coordinates with you and your bridesmaids is perfect. Or, he can skip the suit and tie and wear a linen shirt with a vest, a nice pair of pants, and sandals instead. Always keep your casual, relaxed aesthetic in mind.

## ring bearer & flower girl

Flower girls love to dress up. Give her a dress with ruffles, a petticoat, and material that will twirl around her when she spins, and she will be one very happy member of the wedding party. A crown of some sort will be a reason for delight, whether it's a floral wreath or a sequined tiara.

The handmade, soft-soled shoes below are from Bitsy Blossom and are available in sizes 0 to 13 (for both girls and boys). The very dapper ring bearer's pair is made with gray fabric and a touch of black faux leather with lace-up ties. The flower girl's shoes are made of gold and off-white fabric, embellished with a beautiful, oversized bow with a touch of bling on top.

# The Flowers

Flowers for a boho-style wedding are typically of the "vintage" variety. They are longtime favorites, such as peonies, heritage roses, daisies, hellebores, hydrangeas, etc. Romantic and feminine, they are sometimes offset with an eccentric touch. Spiky blue sea holly is one nontraditional choice, as is the strangely beautiful green amaranth — ideal for a cascade affect. They both represent the casual ease of boho-style flowers.

## bouquets

The bridal bouquet is the heart and soul of wedding flowers. After you've selected your dress, you can decide which flowers will complement it the best. The floral varieties noted above can be paired with miniature daisies, carnations, and baby's breath. However, they don't have to just play a supporting role — no longer considered "filler" flowers, they can take center stage and hold their own.

## boutonnieres

I love boutonnieres; they are the little gems of flower arranging. Want to try making a few for your groom and his groomsmen? You'll need two or three flowers and a stem of greenery for each boutonniere, a pair of scissors, floral tape, wire cutters, and boutonniere pins.

First, strip off any leaves from the stems and wrap three with floral tape. If you want to add a ribbon or twine "cover," now's the time. Determine how long you want the boutonniere to be and trim the stems with the wire cutters. Use the boutonniere pin to attach it to the left lapel. If possible, make some boutonnieres ahead of time and keep them in the refrigerator to test how long they last — some florals are going to be more fragile than others.

# The Reception

What do you have in mind for a reception? The party of the year? An unforgettable event? A quiet gathering of close friends and family? These are just a few of the questions for both of you to consider. The "standard" reception can be daunting, but if you've got some support and, most important, some time, you can combine elements from all of the above and have the reception of your dreams.

## welcoming your guests

Welcome guests to your reception with warmth and a genuine appreciation that they are a part of this extraordinarily special day. As they enter the space, friends and family will be delighted to see a "memory walk" of photographs and memorabilia from your early days when dating, your holidays together with family, or your childhoods. A nice touch is to set aside a special place to honor friends and family who are no longer with you. At the end of the walk, have bottles of water, glasses of punch, and signature cocktails ready to drink, along with bite-size nibbles. Provide a lounge area where guests can mingle and sit on sofas and upholstered chairs, while enjoying the appetizers.

## escort cards, table numbers & place cards

Escort cards are another way to bring your theme into your printed material. Make them yourself or ask your designer to include them in your invitation suite.

If you choose to make them yourself, this can be a fun task. You can use paper, vintage postcards, maps, fabric, lace, or pages from a book you both love, and add a motif, your initials, or the wedding date. Write the guest's name and the table number, and display the cards in an easy-to-find spot by the entrance to your reception. You can also work the same design and/or materials into the table numbers — just make them visible enough to be seen across a room.

If you're placing personal thank-you notes or favors at each setting, you may want to use place cards. A place card designates which seat the guest is "assigned." Set the card with the guest's name at the correct table settings.

## decor

If you both love vintage furniture, turn that passion into a treasure hunt for items to decorate the venue with a personal touch. A small antique table or desk is a perfect place to collect cards from your guests, to setup the guest book, or to display wedding favors. Crystal or antique chandeliers and distressed-wood cupboards or boxes would also add to the boho vibe.

Signs are always helpful — I love the simplicity of the sparkly gold arrow and the inventiveness of the door-turned-chalkboard-sign, below left and right.

You can turn an old door into a chalkboard sign by painting over the panel with chalkboard paint (Rust-Oleum makes chalkboard paint in a brush-on formula). Use chalk to write a personalized greeting for guests, display your menu, or list table assignments.

## TABLE DECOR

For a boho-style wedding, chairs and tables are often white, a classic and elegant look that complements any color palette you choose.

To lay a pretty foundation, look for white or ivory tablecloths made from cotton, linen or lace (for a layered look). Crave color? Opt for muted or bleached pastels and vintage floral tablecloths. Borrow vintage table linens from your grandmother, mother, or aunt. Or, browse thrift stores — a gold mine of boho-style decor.

Mismatched china designs add a whimsical flair; try floral or pastel patterns. You'll also want to look for china with gold trim — a frequent feature of boho table settings.

You can buy or rent vintage china plates for your reception tables. (Online, check out Vintage Plate Rental for the Unites States, or Vintage Dish Rental for Canada.) Place silver flatware and a china plate at each guest's table setting, with a decorative menu and cloth napkin arranged on top.

### CENTERPIECES

For your centerpieces, look for items that will enhance your boho-style blooms. For example, decorate with vintage floral handkerchiefs, votive candles, lace doilies, and mercury glass (candleholders and vases). If you can't find mercury glass at any thrift stores, try a home-goods store, such as World Market.

You'll also want to look for milk glass — also called "opaque glass" — which is traditionally opaque white in color and features textured, raised "dots" across the exterior surface. Genuine milk glass is expensive and considered a collectible item, as it is made with porcelain. If you find milk glass at a thrift store, it is most likely a reproduction. However, genuine and faux versions look surprisingly similar. You can also search eBay or browse estate sales for milk-glass bottles and vases.

Vintage bottles make beautiful table decor, especially in gentle shades, like pale blue. Add water and a few floral stems to create a romantic vase.

A vintage pillar candleholder doesn't have to hold a candle — you could place a single, softly colored flower bloom on top instead.

## the sweetheart table

The sweetheart table for the newlywed couple is akin to thrones for a king and queen. Celebrate yourselves and the beginning of your new life together with a special table just for the two of you. Place it front and center, or even elevated on a platform, and enjoy the toasts and good wishes from your family and friends.

Distinguish your place of honor with two chairs that are completely different from the guests' seating. Your tablecloth, napkins, and table decor can also be unique and special. Of course, you must add the obligatory signs identifying you as the "Bride" and "Groom" or "Mr." and "Mrs."

## guest book

A guest book is an essential keepsake of signatures and well wishes from your guests. Place your guest book — or guest-book alternative — on a table in a well-lit area, with plenty of pens or markers.

Love the classic guest book? A simple blank journal with a linen cover ties in beautifully with boho-chic decor, and it is easy to find at a craft or stationery store.

If you'd rather use an alternative to a traditional guest book, there are many charming options. To make a "tree" guest book, purchase a tree print (from an Etsy shop such as By Yolanda or Trees Please Paintings) with blank leaves onto which guests can sign their names. After the wedding, you can frame and display the print in your home.

A wooden monogram letter is another unique alternative. An unfinished-wood letter can be purchased from a craft store and painted. Guests can sign their names onto the wood with a fine-point permanent marker.

Before signing, guests will love to flip through a photo-album guest book. Upload photos from your courtship to an online photo company (like Shutterfly, for instance) and order a custom photo book. Leave room on the pages for guests to sign their names anywhere they wish.

## card box

It's always thoughtful to provide a place for guests to leave cards. But instead of a traditional card box, use an old, "artfully" weathered container, such as a milk crate, birdcage, mailbox, or suitcase. For a do-it-yourself project, buy a vintage suitcase and adorn it with antique lace. String bunting across and stencil the word "cards" on the fabric or you can make lightweight letters from card stock paint them, and add glitter to spell out "cards" that way. Attach to the lining with miniature clothespins as seen in this photograph at right.

## wedding favors

While browsing shops for reception decor, you can also look for items that can be used as wedding favors. For example, vintage china teacups make charming tokens for guests. At a friend's wedding, each guest's table setting included a teacup in a whimsical pattern, filled with bags of herbal tea.

Or, gift your guests with a few of your favorite teas, placed in stamped muslin bags (or with "thank you" tags attached).

One of my favorite homemade wedding favors is a lavender sachet. Lavender sachets are scented, aromatic "pillows" or bags that you place in a drawer or closet. To make your own sachets, buy dried lavender or potpourri from a craft store and place it in small, unbleached-cotton drawstring bags. Or, sew pillows from two 10 inch squares of pretty, patterned cotton and two 10 inch squares of linen. Place one-third cup of lavender on one linen square, place the other linen square on top, and sew all four corners. Then, place the linen pillow on one square of cotton, place the other cotton square on top, and sew the four corners. Pair two sachets together and wrap them in twine, ready for gifting to guests.

Guests always welcome edible wedding favors, like cookies packaged in white kraft-paper bags with a custom sticker seal. Another suggestion is homemade jelly or jam, placed in canning jars with a personalized label printed from your computer.

Homemade bars of soap — wrapped in pretty paper — or homemade candles in mason jars are also delightful favors that guests will take home and enjoy.

## the cake

A boho-themed wedding is the perfect setting for a romantic, fantasy-style cake. After all, wedding cake is what dreams are made of: delicious, sugary fondant, creamy icing, and detailing that is almost too pretty to eat (almost — it's still cake!).

I adore the look of a "ribbon cake," with icing that is piped on to resemble rows of elegant ribbons, and pink flower buds for a pretty finishing touch.

A sponge cake made with layers of icing can be placed on a cake stand and topped with sweet, edible sugar roses.

A square or rectangle cake is made even more elegant with cascading flowers across several tiers and softly hued ribbons from your color palette.

How will you top the cake? A cute way to add a personalized touch to your wedding cake is by customizing a pair of wooden figurines to look like you and the groom. At any craft store, you can buy wooden figurines, a round wooden base, paint, and fabric details (look in the doll aisle for accessories like miniature bow ties or dresses). For the bride's veil, cut a piece of tulle and attach a rhinestone detail; for her bouquet, use small craft flowers. Set the couple atop an embellished "stand" — a simple, round piece of wood covered in satin fabric.

When you're ready to cut the cake, do it in style. This beautiful serving set, right, features handles that look like small tree branches with a gold-color finish. The cake server and knife will be treasured and can be used over and over again in your new home.

For charming cupcake toppers (or skewers for hors d'oeuvres), use toothpicks and white paper to make tiny flags. Fold a piece of paper in half to make a crease; use scissors to cut triangles from the crease to make wraparound triangle "flags." Place the toothpick in the crease of your triangle flag, apply a dab of glue, and press down to glue the toothpick to the paper. Decorate each flag by adding a stamp in colored ink — use your initials or a heart shape, for example.

## DESSERT BAR

Finally, offer guests a tasty after-dinner treat by setting up a dessert bar. A dessert bar can be used in lieu of wedding cake, and it should be stocked with delicacies like cupcakes, pies, cookies, brownies, and any other sweets that you'd like.

Your dessert bar doesn't have to be elaborate. One of my favorite dessert-bar ideas is to serve chocolate-chip cookies and small glasses of milk — simple, popular, and surprisingly boho-chic!

If you'd prefer to turn the dessert table into a grand display, decorate it with a floral or lace tablecloth, bunting garland (to read something like "Love Is Sweet"), and vintage-china cake plates. Look for antique, tarnished cake servers and tongs for guests to use. If you wish, the dessert bar can also supply your wedding favors — simply provide white to-go bags or boxes. Just make sure that the items you serve are in to-go sizes and are easy to place in a to-go container.

# Resources

Page 255

Blue Magpie / www.bluemagpieinvitations.com;

Hoopla Love / www.etsy.com/shop/hooplalove;

Jen Simpson Design / www.jensimpsondesign.com

Page 257

IKEA / www.ikea.com;

Etsy / www.etsy.com

Page 261

Rust-Oleum / www.rustoleum.com;

Teresa's Plants & More / www.etsy.com/shop/teresasplants;

Superior Craft Supply / www.superiorcraftsupply

Page 264

Mignonne Handmade / mignonnehandmade.com;

J. Crew / jcrew.com;

Free People / www.freepeople.com;

Aya Bridal / www.etsy.com/shop/AyaBridal;

Atelier Signature / www.etsy.com/shop/ateliersignature

Page 265

Bitsy Blossom / www.etsy.com/shop/bitsyblossom

Page 272

Vintage Plate Rental (U.S.) / www.vintageplaterental.com;

Vintage Dish Rental (Canada) / www.vintagedishrental.com

Page 273

World Market / www.worldmarket.com

Page 276

By Yolanda / www.etsy.com/shop/ByYolanda;

Trees Please Paintings / www.etsy.com/shop/TreesPleasePaintings;

Shutterfly / www.shutterfly.com

# Afterwords

These pages may have come to an end, but your story has just begun. I hope the themes and handcrafted details outlined in this book have helped to pave the way for your dream wedding, and that you'll have the special day you've always envisioned. Cherish every minute of it. Most of all, I hope you find an abundance of joy in your new life ahead!

-E.

# Credits

The Publisher wishes to thank the following for permission to reproduce images All credits are noted clockwise from the top right.

**Abbreviation key:** TL (top left), TC (top center), TR (top right), CL (center left), C (center), CR (center right), BL (bottom left), BC (bottom center), BR (bottom right).

**Interior Photo Credits:**

p. 2 © 2014 Michelle Gardella Photography www.michellegardella.com. **p. 5** © 2014 Katherine Clark Photography http://www.katherineclarkphotography.com. **p. 6** TL © 2014 Eric Boneske Photography www.ericboneskephotography.com, CL © 2014 Michelle Gardella Photography, CR © 2014 Michelle Gardella Photography, BL © 2014 Justin Battenfield http://justinbattenfield.com. **p. 7** TL © 2014 Carolyn Scott Photography www.carolynscottphotography.com, CR © 2014 Carolyn Scott Photography, CL © 2014 Carolyn Scott Photography, BR © 2014 Michelle Gardella Photography. **p. 8** © 2014 Carolyn Scott Photography. **p. 9** © 2014 Wood & Grain www.woodandgrain.com. **pp. 11-16** © 2014 Michelle Gardella Photography. **p. 17** TR © 2014 Michelle Gardella Photography, BR © 2014 Jen Simpson Design www.jensimpsondesign.com, BL © 2014 Ello There www.etsy.com/shop/ElloThere. **p. 18** © 2014 Jen Simpson Design. **p. 19** © 2014 Amanda Day Rose www.amandadayrose.com. **pp. 20-24** © 2014 Michelle Gardella Photography. **p. 25** TR © 2014 Michelle Gardella Photography, BL © 2014 Miniature Rhino, www.miniaturerhino.etsy.com. **pp. 26-29** © 2014 Michelle Gardella Photography. **p. 30** TR © 2014 Michelle Gardella Photography, BR © 2014 Emici Bridal www.etsy.com/shop/EmiciBridal, BC © 2014 Michelle Gardella Photography, BL © 2014 Michelle Gardella Photography, TL © 2014 Michelle Gardella Photography. **p. 31** TC © 2014 Justin Battenfield, BR © 2014 Michelle Gardella Photography, BL © 2014 Michelle Gardella Photography. **p. 32** BC © 2014 Justin Battenfield, TL © 2014 Michelle Gardella Photography. **p. 33** © 2014 Michelle Gardella Photography.**p. 34** TC © 2014 Michelle Gardella Photography, BR© 2014 Michelle Gardella Photography, BL © 2014 Justin Battenfield. **pp. 35-36** © 2014 Michelle Gardella Photography **p. 37** TC © 2014 Michelle Gardella Photography, BL © 2014 Carolyn Scott Photography. **p. 38** © 2014 Michelle Gardella Photography. **p. 39** © 2014 Carolyn Scott Photography. **pp. 40-42** © 2014 Michelle Gardella Photography. **p. 43** TR © 2014 Michelle Gardella Photography, C © 2014 Michelle Gardella Photography, BR © 2014 Michelle Gardella Photography, TL © 2014 Mavora Art and Design. **p. 44** TR © 2014 Michelle Gardella Photography, BR © 2014 Michelle Gardella Photography, BC BR © 2014 Michelle Gardella Photography, BL © 2014 Carolyn Scott Photography, TL © 2014 Michelle Gardella Photography. **p. 45** © 2014 Michelle Gardella Photography. **p. 46** © 2014 Michelle Gardella Photography. **p. 47** CR © 2014 Carolyn Scott Photography, BL © 2014 Michelle Gardella Photography. **pp. 48-52** © 2014 Michelle Gardella Photography. **pp. 54-55** © 2014 Justin Battenfield. **p. 56** © 2014 Amanda Day Rose. **p. 57** © 2014 Wood and Grain. **p. 58** TC © 2014 Michelle Gardella Photography, BR © 2014 Amanda Day Rose. **p. 59** © 2014 Amanda Day Rose. **p. 60** TR © 2014 Wood and Grain, BR © 2014 Jen Simpson Design, TL © 2014 Wood and Grain. **p. 61** © 2014 Justin Battenfield. **pp. 62-66** © 2014 Michelle Gardella Photography. **p. 67** TR © 2014 Carolyn Scott Photography, BL © 2014 Michelle Gardella Photography. **pp. 68-69** © 2014 Michelle Gardella Photography. **p. 70** BR © 2014 Carolyn Scott Photography, TL © 2014 Michelle Gardella Photography. **p. 71** TR © 2014 Melania Marta Photography, BL © 2014 Justin Battenfield, TL © 2014 Michelle Gardella Photography. **p. 72-74** © 2014 Michelle Gardella Photography. **p. 75** TC © 2014 Michelle Gardella Photography, BR © 2014 Kristin Coffin Jewelry, www.kristincoffin.com. **p. 76** TC © 2014 Justin Battenfield, BC © 2014 Michelle Gardella Photography. **p. 77** TR © 2014 Michelle Gardella Photography, BC © 2014 Justin Battenfield. **pp. 78-81** © 2014 Michelle Gardella Photography. **p. 82** © 2014 Lynn P. Smith. **p. 83** TR © 2014 Michelle Gardella Photography, BL© 2014 Carolyn Scott Photography, TR © 2014 Michelle Gardella Photography. **pp. 84-85** © 2014 Michelle Gardella Photography. **p. 86** TC © 2014 Carolyn Scott Photography, BR © 2014 Michelle Gardella Photography. **pp. 87-90** © 2014 Michelle Gardella Photography. **p. 91** © 2014 Justin Battenfield. **pp. 92-93** © 2014 Michelle Gardella Photography. **p. 94** TR © 2014 Michelle Gardella Photography, BL © 2014 Michelle Gardella Photography, TR © 2014 Wood and Grain, TC © 2014 Wood and Grain. **p. 95** TR © 2014 Carolyn Scott Photography, BC © 2014 Michelle Gardella Photography. **p. 96** BR © 2014 Wood and Grain. BL © 2014 Melania Marta Photography. **p. 97** © 2014 Eric Boneske Photography. **p. 98** TR © 2014 Carolyn Scott Photography, TL © 2014 Michelle Gardella Photography. **pp. 100-101** © 2014 Eric Boneske Photography. **p. 102** © 2014 Michelle Gardella Photography. **p. 103** © 2014 Mavora Art and Design www.mavora.com. **p. 104** TR © 2014 In or Out Media www.etsy.com/shop/starboardpress, BL © 2014 Wide Eyes Design www.etsy.com/shop/WideEyesPaperCo. **p. 105** TC © 2014 In or Out Media, BR © 2014 Serendipity Beyond Design www.serendipitybeyonddesign.com. **p. 106** © 2014 Shillawna Ruffner Photography www.shillawnaruffner.com. **p. 107** TC © 2014 {via} Vacious Design www.etsy.com/shop/viavaciousdesigns, TL © 2014 Amanda Day Rose www.amandadayrose.com. **p. 108** TC © 2014 Amanda Day Rose, BR © 2014 Laura Hooper Calligraphy www.etsy.com/shop/LHCalligraphy. **p. 109** © 2014 Ruff House Art www.ruffhouseart.com. **p. 110** © 2014 Pure 7 Studios www.pure7studios.com. **p. 111** TC © 2014 Michelle Gardella Photography, BR © 2014 Beach Weddings by Bree www.etsy.com/shop/BeachWeddingsByBree. **p. 112** © 2014 Pure 7 Studios. **p. 113** TC © 2014 Melania Marta Photography www.melaniamphotography.com, BR © 2014 Lucky You, Lucky Me www.etsy.com/shop/LuckyYouLuckyMe, BL © 2014 Carolyn Scott Photography. **p. 114** TR © 2014 Eric Boneske Photography, BC © 2014 Michelle Gardella Photography. **p. 115** TR © 2014 Genevieve McKeiver, www.gmckeiverphotography.com, BL © 2014 Eric Boneske Photography. **p. 116** CR © 2014 Eric Boneske Photography, BL © 2014 Shillawna Ruffner Photography, TL © 2014 Carolyn Scott Photography. **p. 117** © 2014 Shillawna Ruffner Photography. **p. 118** CR © 2014 Shillawna Ruffner Photography, BL © 2014 Eric Boneske Photography, TL © 2014 Shillawna Ruffner Photography. **p. 119** TC © 2014 Eric Boneske Photography, BR © 2014 Shillawna Ruffner Photography, BC © 2014 Amy Stewart for Junghwa, BL © 2014 Amy Stewart for Junghwa. **p. 120** © 2014 Eric Boneske Photography. **p. 121** TR © 2014 Genevieve McKeiver, TL © 2014 Eric Boneske Photography. **p. 122** TC © 2014 Eric Boneske Photography, BC © 2014 Shillawna Ruffner Photography. **p. 123** CR © 2014 Eric Boneske Photography, BL © 2014 The Bridal Flower www.thebridalflower.com, CL © 2014 Eric Boneske Photography, C © 2014 Shillawna Ruffner Photography. **p. 124** © 2014 Michelle Gardella Photography. **p. 125** TR © 2014 Shillawna Ruffner Photography, BR © 2014 Fairyfolk Weddings www.etsy.com/shop/FairyfolkWeddings, BC © 2014 The Sunflower Stand www.thesunflowerstand.com, BL © 2014 Eric Boneske Photography, TL © 2014 Shillawna Ruffner Photography. **p. 126** TR © 2014 Carolyn Scott Photography, TL © 2014 Katherine Clark Photography. **p. 127** TR © 2014 Steve Steinhardt www.stevesteinhardt.com, BR © 2014 Michelle Gardella Photography, BL © 2014 Jennifer Skog www.jenniferskog.com. **p. 128** TR © 2014 Michelle Gardella Photography, C © 2014 Shillawna Ruffner Photography. **p. 129** TR © 2014 Genevieve McKeiver, BC © 2014 Eric Boneske Photography. **p. 130** TR © 2014 Eric Boneske Photography, C © 2014 Carolyn Scott Photography. **p. 131** © 2014 Eric Boneske Photography. **p. 132** TC © 2014 Eric Boneske Photography, BR © 2014 Shillawna Ruffner Photography. **p. 133** CR © 2014 Michelle Gardella Photography, CL © 2014 Shillawna Ruffner Photography. **p. 134** © 2014 Michelle Gardella Photography. **p. 135** TR © 2014 Eric Boneske Photography, CR © 2014 Katy Biagini www.katybphoto.com, BR © 2014 Shillawna Ruffner Photography, TL © 2014 Shillawna Ruffner Photography, TC © 2014 Shillawna Ruffner Photography. **p. 136** CR © 2014 Michelle Gardella Photography, BC © 2014 Shillawna Ruffner Photography. **p. 138** © 2014 Carolyn Scott Photography. **p. 140** © 2014 Jen Simpson Design. **p. 141** TR © 2014 Serendipity Beyond Design, BC © 2014 Michelle Gardella Photography, TL © 2014 Daydream Prints www.etsy.com/shop/daydreamprints. **p. 142** © 2014 Hoopla Love www.etsy.com/shop/hooplalove. **pp. 143-145** © 2014 Carolyn Scott Photography. **p. 146** TC © 2014 Justin

Pages in *italic* indicate photos

aisle decor, *256*
  aisle runner providing aisle decor, 224
    *See also* runners
  defining the wedding space, 67–68, 186
  lighting for evening wedding, 257
  providing a vintage feel, 23
  sources for
    Hobby Lobby, 224, 251
    Michaels (craft stores), 224, 251
  tweaking classic customs to be more
    contemporary, 147–48
  use of flowers as accents, 23, *24*
altar as focal point for exchange of vows, 65,
  112, 147, 221, 225
aluminum cans as hanging decor, 90
amaranth as a flower choice, 266
analogous colors, 11
anemones as a flower choice, 123, 239
antiques
  for aisle decor, 23
  for backdrop or focal point, 22
  as a wedding party gift, 26
aquarium as a wedding location, 182–83
arbors as focal point for exchange of vows,
  65–66
  Bamboo Expressions as source of bamboo
    arbor, 112, 137
arches as focal point for exchange of vows, 65,
  112, 145, 225, 259
architectural pieces, use of in design, 22
Art Deco style, 16–17, 26
  Art Deco forever bouquet, 37
art galleries *See* museums and art galleries as
  wedding location
attire, wedding *See also* specific attendants,
  i.e., bridesmaids, ring bearer, etc.,
  Beach Bliss themed ideas, 117–22
  Boho style themed ideas, 262–65
  Farmhouse Rustic themed ideas, 73–78
  Free Spirit themed ideas, 192–98
  Romantically Vintage themed ideas, 28–35
  Traditional Wedding themed ideas, 232–36
  Urban Chic themed ideas, 154–60
aviary as a wedding location, 183

baby's breath as a flower choice, 130, 239, 266
backyard weddings, 20, 61, 62, *62–63*, *185*,
  185, 225
baked goods as guest favors, 94, 248, 277
bandeau veil, 30
banners, use of as decorations, 52, 66, 89–90,
  186, 206
  cake banner, 98
  flower girl or ring bearer carrying, 149, 188
  pennant flags, 71, 214
    Betawife as source for, 188, 215
barns as a motif, 58
  as a possible wedding location, 63, 82
baskets, choices of materials to be made of, 71
  sources for
    Superior Craft Supply, 261, 280
    Teresa's Plants & More, 261, 280
beach as wedding location, 101, 110, 111, 112,
  115, 116, 121, 126, 128, 133, 136, 187, 222
beach roses as a flower choice, 113, 123
bell jar, use of as decorations, 92
best woman, 195
birch, use of as decorations, 88
  birch bark
    birch bark vase, 90–91
    as a cake stand, 96
    for guest book, 93
    pail filled with flowers, 92
  sources for
    Birch Bark Store, 130, 137
    PNZ Designs, 71, 99
    Roxy Heart Vintage, 98, 99
  tree slice used as cupcake stand, 98, 99

birdcage veil, 96, 118, 193
birdcages, use of as decorations, 23, 47, 276
  for centerpieces, 47
  flower girl carrying, 25
  use of as a cardbox, 276
blusher veil, 118
bolero, 73, 118, 155, 264
books, used as decorations, 47
  as centerpieces, 206
  flower girl carrying, 200
  as the guest book, 45
  ring bearer carrying, 189
botanical garden as a wedding location, 183
bouquet toss, 36, 209, 247
bouquets, *38, 39, 81, 100, 124, 162, 201, 237,*
  *237, 238, 239, 266, 267, 268*
  adding a locket with photo to honor a
    loved one who has passed away, 123
  alternatives to, 37, 79, 80, 123, 125, 162,
    200, *201*
  coordinated with groomsmen's
    boutonniers, 235
  dried-flower bouquets, 80
  handles for bouquets, *38, 123,* 162
    creating homemade handles for,
      80, 193
    The Little Red Button as source for, 162,
      175
  nautical theme, 123
  nostalgic flower choices, 37
  ways to reflect a specific era, 36–38
boutonniers, *38,* 38, *125, 162, 163, 199, 200,*
  *268*
  alternatives to flowers, 125, 162, 199, 200
  handcrafted, 80
  coordinated with bouquets, 38, 80, 125,
    163, 235, 239
  making your own, 199–200, 268
  sources for
    Fairyfolk Weddings, 125, 137
    The Little Red Button, 162, 175
    Michelle's Clay Creations, 199, 215
    She Wore White, 199, 215
    The Sunflower Stand, 125, 137
    When Geeks Wed, 199, 215
boxes, wooden, 70, 148, 172
braids as a rustic look for bride, 74
breakfast-themed reception, 202
brewery as a wedding location, 183
bridal gown and accessories, *106, 263*
  adding accessories to reflect theme and
    personality, 193
  adding rustic flair, 79–81
  asking family members for use of gown or
    accessories, 29
  avoiding fabrics and styles from bygone
    days, 154
  casual choices for a beach wedding,
    117–18
  choosing for a traditional wedding, 233–34
  gown serving as inspiration for wedding
    flowers, 161
  pants instead of bridal gown, 263
  pointers for shopping for, 262
  reflecting your personality and boho style,
    262–64
  sources for
    BHLDN, 28, 53
    The Dessy Group, 117
    eBay, 28, 53
    Etsy, 28, 53
    Ruche, Inc., 28, 53
  traditions relating to, 232
  unconventional choices for free-spirit
    wedding, 192–94
  vintage wedding attire, 28–30
bride, *5, 14, 28, 29, 34, 52, 54, 70, 102, 117,*
  *136, 138, 144, 153, 154, 157, 176, 184, 187,*
  *192, 202, 218, 221, 223, 252, 254, 281*
bridesmaid(s), *262*

attire, sources for
  Atelier Signature, 264, 280
  Aya Bridal, 264, 280
  Fleet Collection, 34, 53
  Free People, 264, 280
  J. Crew, 264, 280
  ModCloth, 34, 53
  Muse Bridal Wear, 157, 175
attire, *33, 156, 157, 158*
  allowing variety, 194, 264
  focusing on silhouette, 155, 157
  unconventional choices for free-spirit
    wedding, 194–95
  ways to reflect a specific era, 32, 34
  gifts for, 26, 34, 72, 150–51, 230
  choosing different gifts to match
    different personalities, 190
brooches, creative uses of, 25, 27, 30, 227
  brooch bouquet, 37
    The Ritzy Rose as a source for, 37, 53
buckets, use of as decorations, 23, 68
  flower girl carrying, 25, 71
  to hold ceremony program, 70
bugs at outdoor weddings, 67, 116
burlap for texture, 68, 71, 257
  used as aisle decorations, Burlap Pew
    Cones as source for, 224, 251
butterfly house as a wedding location, 183
buttons, pin-back as favors, Big Yellow Dog
  Designs as a source for, 173, 175

cake topper ideas, 50, *96, 98, 174,* 174, 213,
  *213,* 213, 250, *278,* 278–79 *See also* wedding
  cake
  adirondack chairs, 135, 137
  sources for
    Dream Cake Toppers, 174
    Goose Grease, 50, 53
    Julie the Fish Designs, 174
    Knottingwood, 50, 53
    Lulu's Little Shop, 174
    Lynn's Little Creations, 250, 251
    The Pink Owl Designs, 250, 251
    Rustic Blend, 135, 137
    By the Seashore Decor as source for,
      135, 137
    Wood & Grain, 96, 99
calla lillies as a flower choice, 123, 148, 239
calligraphy, Laura Hooper Calligraphy as source
  for, 108, 127, 137
candleholders, pillar, 273
candles, 169
  battery operated, 67, 88–89, 111, 206
  as favors for guests, 277
    Beach Weddings by Bree as source for,
      136, 137
  floating candles as centerpieces, 170
  votive candles, 91–92
candy
  candy buffet, 172, 174
    Candy Warehouse as source for, 95,
      99, 135–36, 137
  chocolate seashell candies, Andie's
    Specialty Sweets as source for, 135, 137
  as favors for guests, 49, 95, 172, 210
    Jordan almonds tradition, 247
    sea-glass candy, 135
  use of as escort cards, Peeps as source for,
    203, 215
card box, 44, 70, 276, *276*
  an antique table or desk instead, 271
caricature artist at reception, 173
cedar pilings, Nautical Seasons as source for,
  132, 137
cell phones, asking to power down, 153
centerpieces, *47, 47, 48,* 48, 49, *274 See also*
  table decor
  "Eiffel Tower" vase, 245, *246,* 251
  minimalist centerpieces, 170
  rustic-wedding choices, 90–92

setting a relaxed mood with, 129–30, *131*
sources for
  Save-on-Crafts as source for, 245, 251
  World Marker, 273, 280
"submerged" centerpieces, 245
unconventional choices for free-spirit
  wedding, 206
vintage items lending boho style, 273
ceremony, wedding, 61–81
  Beach Bliss themed ideas, 110–16
  Boho style themed ideas, 256–61
  choosing unconventional locations for,
    182–83
  escorting the bride, 187, 227
  Farmhouse Rustic themed ideas, 61–81
  Free Spirit themed ideas, 182–91
  music for, 228
  providing transportation from ceremony to
    reception, 152
  readings at, 186
  Romantically Vintage themed ideas, 20–27
  seeing each other before the ceremony,
    187
  traditions for, 146, 227–28, 234, 247
    dances, 247
    getting-ready tradition, 234
    nontraditional traditions, 187
    pearls as traditional bride choice, 233
    relating to choice of bridal gown, 232
    relating to the wedding cake, 250
    relating to transportation, 231
  Urban Chic themed ideas, 143–53
ceremony program, 13, 25, 70, 114, 149, 225
  format choices, 25
  placement of, 114
  sources for
    Beacon Lane, 225, 251
    Hoopla Love, 149, 175
    Lama Works, 225, 251
  suggested content for, 149, 225
    including readings in, 186
    including vows in, 70
chalkboards, 12
  as a cake topper, Gartner Studios as a
    source for, 96, 99
  to display ceremony program, 114
  to display seating guidelines, 85, 204, *204*
  offering personalized greetings to guests,
    271
  Rust-Oleum as source for chalkboard paint,
    271, 280
chandeliers, use of in design, 22, 89
  to add formal feel to a tented reception,
    241
chuppah as focal point for exchange of vows,
  65, 112, 145, 147, 221, 223
cigar bar, 249
cigar cutter as gift for groomsmen, 151
cigars as gifts for groomsmen, 72
cloche, use of as decorations, 92
clothespins, use of as decorations
  to create an escort card display, 85, 165
  to display photos from photo booth, 208
  Factory Direct Craft as source for, 43, 53
clutch bags or totes, 152
  sources for
    Allisa Jacobs, 150, 175
    Angee W., 230, 251
cocktail hour/bar, *41,* 242
  choosing vintage cocktails, 40
  food selections for, 128
  ways to make rustic, 82–83
coffee mugs as favors, Anthropoloigie as source
  for, 49, 53
coffee tin, use of as decorations, 23, 25, 49
coloring as a kid's activity at reception, 173
  The Coloring Spot as source for, 133, 137
colors
  choosing a color palette, 11–12, 16, 76,
    104

all white palette, 167
for a beach theme, 104
black and white color palette, 158
for a nautical theme, 104
for rustic-farmhouse theme, 58
contemporary colors, 155
inventive ways to use color in table decor, 132
ombre style, 158
as aisle runner, 147
in ring pillow, 148
Sparkle Soiree source for colored silk petals, 147, 175
comic-book themed wedding, 209
computer games as a wedding theme, 179, 179
matching wedding party gifts to theme, 190
confetti
making your own, 175
sources for
Flower Fetti, 148, 153, 175, 224, 251
Mavora Art and Design as source for bags to hold, 153, 175
used to decorate aisle, 224
cookies as favors for guests, 248, 277
corkboard to display escort cards, 203
corsages, 80, 161, 162, 163, 239 See also flowers
cottage near a lake as a wedding location, 126, 256
cowboy boots as a motif, 58
craspedia as a flower choice, 162, 163, 170
crates, use of as decorations, 44, 67, 70, 91, 92, 276
cupcakes, 98, 174, 213, 279
cupcake toppers, 279
as theme for a guest book, 205
customs, wedding, 227–28
getting-ready tradition, 234
nontraditional traditions, 187
pearls as traditional bride choice, 233
relating to choice of bridal gown, 232
relating to the wedding cake, 250
relating to transportation, 231
traditional dances, 248–49

daisies as a flower choice, 79, 239, 260
dancing at reception, 52, 126, 143, 145, 173, 207, 208
choosing songs to encourage dancing, 249
dance floor
decorating the floor itself, 169
illuminating, 167
props for, 208
traditions for specific dances, 248–49
dessert bar, 172, 174, 250, 258
use of in lieu of wedding cake, 279
desserts, as favors for guests, 248
destination weddings, timing for mailings, 12, 56, 254
dinosaur theme for a wedding
Dinosaur encyclopedia serving as guest book, 205
dinosaur footprints as decorations, 186
ring bearer carrying figurine, 188–89
Doctor Who as a wedding theme, 190, 192, 196
dog at the wedding, 184, 265
Little Blue Feathers as source for bow for dog, 148, 175
doughnuts served instead of wedding cake, 213

earrings, 26, 30, 72, 118, 155, 228, 230, 233, 263
e-mail, use of for RSVPs, 107
embroidery hoop, use of as decoration
for carrying rings, 25
Miniature Rhino as a source for, 25, 53
Emmaline Bride (blog), 9–10, 57, 178, 215
engagement photo, use of for save-the-date, 102
entertainment, 136, 173, 248–49
teaching knot tying, 133
unconventional choices for free-spirit wedding, 207–8
escort cards, 12, 42–43, 84–86, 127
sources for
Hoopla Love, 165, 175
Laura Hooper Calligraphy, 127, 137
Peeps, 203, 215

Washi Tape, 203, 215
use of favors, 43, 49, 127
usefulness of, 203–4
escorting the bride, 187, 227
Etsy, 28, 32, 50, 53, 57, 70, 99, 111, 146, 148, 153, 189, 190, 199, 215, 224, 230, 231, 257, 264, 276, 280
eucalyptus as a flower choice, 65, 79, 162

factory as site for a reception, 165
carrying palm leaf raffia fan instead of bouquet, 125, 137
sources for
Beau Coup, 116, 137
Luna Bazaar, 116, 137
Oriental Trading, 125, 137
farmhouse as a motif, 60
as a possible wedding location, 61, 82
favors, 94, 95
donations to charity instead of favors, 173
edible favors, 43, 49, 94–95, 135, 172, 248, 277
Jordan almonds tradition, 247
providing to-go bags or boxes at dessert bar, 279
functional and useful, 49, 135–36
plants that serve as table decor and favors, 170, 172
sources for
Beach Weddings by Bree, 136, 137
Big Yellow Dog Designs, 173
Candy Warehouse, 136, 137
Latika Soap, 136
Pez dispensers, 210, 215
Soap Cafe, 136, 137
Vice & Velvet, 172, 175
unconventional choices, 209–10
use of as escort cards, 43, 49, 127
use of as place cards, 88
feathers, 125, 255
in bouquets or boutonniers, 80, 125, 200
in a centerpiece, 92
in hair accessories, 30, 118, 193, 195
tossing instead of flowers, 147
felt
in bouquets or boutonniers, 80, 200
felt heart as a cake topper, 174
felt pom poms as aisle decorations, 186
lining for box that substitutes for ring pillow, 189
in wand for flower girl to carry, 71
ferns, use of as decoration, 37, 74, 257
fingertip veil, 264
"first dance," 247
flower girl, 121, 236, 260, 265
attire, sources for
Bitsy Blossom, 265, 280
Olive & Fern, 121, 137, 160, 175
attire for
choosing a "spinnable" outfit, 78, 265
coordinated with bridesmaids' attire, 160, 198
ways to reflect a specific era, 35
gifts for, 27, 72, 152, 231
having more than one, 113, 149
role in a traditional wedding, 229
unconventional choices to carry, 140, 188–89
beach themed items, 113
rustic themed items, 71
vintage themed items, 25
ways to incorporate a young child, 229
flowers See also bouquets; boutonniers; corsages
as accents along aisle, 23, 24
Beach Bliss themed ideas, 123–25
Boho style themed ideas, 266–68
Farmhouse Rustic themed ideas, 79–81
Free Spirit themed ideas, 199–201
Romantically Vintage themed ideas, 36–38
sources for flower alternatives
The Bridal Flower, 123, 137
The Little Red Button, 125, 137
Ribbon and Bows Oh My!, 123, 137
Roxy Heart Vintage, 66, 99
Traditional Wedding themed ideas, 237–39
Urban Chic themed ideas, 161–63
wooden vases for, Heirloom Woodwork as source for, 130, 137

food for the reception, 211
BBQ buffet, 211
breakfast-themed reception, 202, 211
food truck, 202
games at the reception
beach games, 133
board games, 51, 207
computer games as a free-spirited theme, 179
Jenga, 202
lawn games, 84, 207
garden weddings, 20, 222, 256
garlands as decorations, 92, 279
hanging garlands, 22, 66, 90, 133, 167
ring bearers or flower girls carrying, 113, 149
table garlands, 79, 92, 98
garter removal and toss, 207, 209, 247
making an "heirloom" garter, 30
gazebo as part of wedding ceremony, 222, 225
geek chic as a wedding theme, 180, 180, 196, 209, 210
"ghost chair," 146–47
gifts See favors; wedding party, gifts for
glasses as gifts, The Wedding Gallery by Brad Goodell as a source for, 231, 251
gothic/Halloween as a wedding theme, 189, 192, 193, 194, 195
grand exit/send off, 136, 175, 214, 250
grapevines, use of as decorations, 65, 71, 88, 89, 92, 96
used in hair crown, 74
graphic novels as a wedding theme, 179
groom, 5, 32, 34, 52, 54, 70, 102, 117, 136, 138, 144, 153, 154, 158, 176, 184, 187, 200, 202, 218, 221, 223, 252, 254
attire for
casual choices for, 122, 265
importance of comfort and personal preference, 158–59
rustic looks, 76, 76
traditional and "modern" traditional choices, 235
unconventional choices for free-spirit wedding, 196, 196–97
ways to reflect a specific era, 31–32
groom's cake, 175, 213
groomsmen
attire for, 34, 159
casual choices for, 122, 122, 265
rustic looks, 76, 78
unconventional choices, 197
ways to reflect a specific era, 35
coordinated with groom's attire, 235
gifts for, 27, 72, 151, 190, 231
guest book, 45
alternatives to, 93, 129, 171, 205, 205, 207, 244
becoming a 3-D work of art, 171
interactive guest book, 45
sources for
Shutterfly, 276, 280
Suzy Shoppe, 171, 175
Trees Please Paintings, 276, 280
By Yolanda, 276, 280
thumbprint guest book, 93, 205
traditional guest books, 244, 276
"tree" guest book, 276
using photos as, 129, 171, 276

hair accessories, 30, 74, 78, 118, 155, 193, 194–95, 263–64, 264
halo like hair accessory, 155, 264
sources for
Emici Bridal, 30, 53
Mignonne Handmade, 264, 280
Miss Ruby Sue, 118, 137
hairstyle for the bride, 118, 253, 264 See also bridal gown and accessories
choosing braids, 74
hand mirror as a bridesmaid gift, 150
handfasting ceremony, 187
handkerchiefs, 23
use of with centerpieces, 273
used to create bouquet handle, 38
hangers, customized wooden, Get Hung Up as source for, 230, 251
hanging decor, 90, 167–69, 259 See also

banners, use of as decorations; bunting as decorations
hanging garlands, 22, 66, 90, 133, 167
hatbox, use of as card box, 44
hats for the groom, 32, 196
hay bales, use of as decorations or seating, 67, 69, 185
head table See sweetheart table/head table
headbands, 155, 264
hearts as a motif
as a cake topper, 98
origami hearts, 172
use of as aisle decor, 67
herbs
as flower choices, 79
as guest favors, 94
honor attendants, 195
honoring a loved one who has passed away, 153, 270
adding a locket with photo to bouquet, 123
deceased parent included in invitation, 220
hora (chair dance), 249
horseshoes (game), 84, 133, 207
hotels as reception location choice, 240
hydrangeas as a flower choice, 123, 129, 237, 266

IKEA, 111, 115
"in memory of," 153, 270
adding a locket with photo to bouquet, 123
deceased parent included in invitation, 220
industrial chic theme, 143, 145
invitations, 16–17, 254–55
custom invitations, 57–60
examples of, 179, 180, 181, 219, 255
free-spirited themes reflected in, 178–80
items included in, 12, 57, 107
mailing schedule, 12
make your own, 57
sources for
Amanda Day Rose, 57, 58, 59, 99
Blue Magpie Invitations, 255, 280
Crafty Pie Press, 180, 215
Daydream Prints, 141, 175
Ello There, 17, 53
Hoopla Love, 142, 175, 255, 280
Jen Simpson Design, 60, 99, 141, 175, 219, 251, 255, 280
LetterBoxInk, 100, 215
M3 and Co., 179, 215
Ruff House Art, 179, 215
Serendipity Beyond Design, 105, 137, 141, 175
Shine Wedding Invitations, 219, 251
Sparkvites, 180, 215
{via}vacious Designs, 107, 137
Wood & Grain, 57, 60, 99
suggested wording for, 220
traditional and "modern" traditional choices, 218–20
irises as a flower choice, 239
island wedding and need for ferry, 261

jam or jellies as a guest favor, 94, 277
Jenga, guests signing Jenga pieces, 206
jewelry
acorn charm, 75
anchor pendant, 119
Art Deco style, 26
choosing pieces to give rustic feel, 75
estate sales, 19, 32
as gifts for the wedding party, 26, 27, 72, 119, 151, 152, 190, 230, 231
for the groom, 31
incorporating starfish and shells, 119
as an item in "Something Old" tradition, 227, 228, 233
nature inspired, 75
pearls as traditional bride choice, 233
sources for
Erica B. Studios, 190, 215
Junghwa by Amy Stewart, 119, 137
KCowie, 151, 175
Kristin Coffin Jewelry, 75, 99
Kustom Kufflinks, 190, 215
Little Hunny Studio, 72, 99
The Merriweather Council, 152, 175

Spiffing Jewelry, 231, 251
  White Truffle Studio, 231, 251
  use of as decoration, 19, 25
  vintage jewelry, 27, 30
jewelry boxes
  as decorations, 49
  as gifts for the wedding party, 72
Jewish weddings, 223, 228, 249
Juliet cap, 30

keys, use of as decorations, 22, 25, 38, 43,
  47, 49
knots
  knot tying as an activity, 133
  nautical knot bracelet, 119, 119
kraft-paper, use of
  as a choice for stationery, 17, 57, 60
  for escort cards, 86
  for guest book, 93
  kraft-paper bags for favors, 94, 277

lace, 19
  as aisle runners, 23
  in an Art Deco forever bouquet, 37
  use of to create a focal point, 22
lavender
  as favor for guests, 49
  as favors for guests, lavender sachets, 277
  for flower girl to toss, 261
  as a rustic flower choice, 79
LED lighting, 89, 206, 257
lighting
  at the ceremony, 259
  for evening wedding ceremony, 257
  LED lighting, 89, 206, 257
  at the reception, 88–89, 169, 206, 241
  sources for
    IKEA, 257, 280
    Luna Bazaar, 88, 99
linen as choice for aisle runner, 68
locations for reception See venues
lollipops as bouquet, 200
Los Angeles, CA as a wedding location, 143
luggage tags, use of as decorations, 104
  for escort cards, 43
  personalizing, 71
  for save-the-date cards, 103

Mad Libs, customized, 207
magnolias as flower choice, 65
mailbox, aged, use of as card box, 44, 276
mailings
  mailing schedule, 12
  personalizing stamps at Zazzle, 19, 53
  schedule for destination weddings, 12,
    56, 254
man of honor, 195
maps
  to ceremony and reception, 40, 108
  Laura Hooper Calligraphy as source for,
    108, 137
  for out of town guests, 12, 107, 219
  use of as decoration, 243, 255, 270
Marbles Kids Museum (Raleigh, NC), 183, 215
mason-jars
  to hold candles, 111, 127
  mason-jar solar lanterns, 89
  for serving drinks, 128
    used as escort cards, 84–85
  use of to display table numbers, 204
  used as vases, 91–92, 129, 131
"memory walk," 269, 269–70
mercury glass for centerpieces, World Marker
  as source for, 273, 280
monograms See also monograms
  on aisle runners or in aisle decor, 68, 147,
    224, 257
  as cake toppers, 50, 98, 135, 174
  on dance floor, 169
  on gifts, 152, 230
  as guest book alternative, 93, 276
  on invitations, 219
  on ring pillow, 71
  as way to personalize, 12, 88, 167
moss, use of as decoration
  as centerpieces, 90, 92
  moss filled tray to display escort cards, 86
  moss monogram letters, 88
  sources for baskets made of

Superior Craft Supply, 261, 280
  Teresa's Plants & More, 261, 280
  table runners, 91
motifs for themed weddings
  choosing a boho theme, 255
  choosing a rustic-wedding motif, 58–59,
    77
  choosing decorative motifs, 11–12
  choosing vintage motifs, 17, 19
movies as entertainment, 208
Museum of Life + Science (Durham, NC), 183,
  215
museums and art galleries as wedding location,
  20, 145, 182, 183
music See also entertainment
  ceremony music, 228
  at the reception
    play list chosen to match the era, 52
    of a traditional wedding, 248–49
muslin, use of in decorations
  favor bags made of, 49, 135, 277
  to make handle for bouquet, 80
  muslin bag as alternative to ring pillow,
    113, 229
  muslin curtains, 65, 88

napkin rings, making own, 244
National Park Service, 62, 99
national parks as wedding locations, 62
nautical theme, 104, 126–27
  bouquets, 123
  candy buffet, 135
  color palette for, 118
  decorations, 111, 129, 132
  entertainment ideas, 133
  escort cards, 127, 137
  favors for guests, 136
    nautical-knot wine-bottle toppers,
      136
  groom's attire, 122
  guest book, 129
  nautical knot bracelet as a gift, 119, 119
  sources for
    Amanda Day Rose, 107, 137
    Laura Hooper Calligraphy, 127, 137
    Nautical Seasons, 129, 132, 137
    Ribbon and Bows Oh My! 123, 137
    Ruff House Art, 108, 137
    {via}vacious Designs, 106, 137
  stationery, 105, 107, 108, 127, 137
net veil, 264
nontraditional traditions, 187
North Carolina as a location for a beach theme
  wedding, 126

Old Navy, 115
ombre style, 158
  as aisle runner, 147
  in ring pillow, 148
origami
  origami bouquet, 162
  origami cranes, 148, 171
  origami flowers for boutonnieres, 163
  origami hearts, 172
outdoor weddings
  beach weddings, 110–11, 118
  outdoor receptions, 51, 83, 126, 169,
    240, 241
    creating an entryway for reception,
      88–89
    games and activities for, 207–8
  rustic settings, 65–68
  with skyline views, 145
  tented receptions, 20, 46, 63, 126–27, 128,
    145, 240, 241
  thoughtful extras for, 115–16, 185
  use moderation in decorating ceremony
    space, 225
  weather and outdoor weddings, 62, 63,
    115, 126, 145, 222, 241

pails See buckets, use of as decorations
palm fronds, 123
paper flowers, 200
  made from old books, 206
  paper bouquets, 200, 201
    The Little Red Button as source for,
      125, 137
paper lanterns, 169

papier-mâché numbers, use of, 87
parasol, use of as decorations, 186
  flower girl carrying, 113
pearls as traditional bride choice, 233
pennant flags, 71, 214
  Betawife as source for, 188, 215
personalization, 9, 12, 19, 40, 57, 71, 93, 111,
  146, 167, 186, 210, 222, 224, 234
  personalizing favors, 49, 116, 136, 204,
    209, 277
  personalizing gifts to wedding party, 72,
    150, 230, 231
  personalizing the cake, 96, 135, 250, 278
  use of monograms or photos See
    monograms; photos, use of personal
  wedding gown reflecting bride's
    personality, 154, 193, 263
phone covers as gifts, Carved as source for,
  151, 175
photo booths, 51, 133, 171, 173, 208–9, 276
  photos from serving as favors, 173
  props for, 51, 171, 208, 208–9
photos, use of personal, 12, 16
  as aisle decorations, 224
  creating a "memory walk," 269
  as the guest book, 171, 276
    invite guests to sign a favorite photo,
      129
    at the reception for guests to sign on
      the matting, 171
  as part of focal point for exchange of
    vows, 66
  personalizing stamps at Zazzle, 19, 53
  sources for
    Shutterfly, 276, 280
    Snapfish, 171
  in stationery suite, 58, 102
  use of as gifts for wedding party, 72, 230
  use of vintage photos, 22
  on wedding cake, 213
pillbox hat, 30
pinecones
  as aisle decorations, 257
  in bouquet, 80
  in centerpieces, 90, 92
  use of as place cards and favors, 88
pinwheels
  as aisle decorations, 186
  as centerpieces, 206
  flower girl carrying, 188, 200
  pinwheels instead of bouquet, 200
    Pinwhirls as source for, 125, 137
place cards, 12, 86, 166, 204, 243, 270
  combining place cards with favors, 88
  making your own, 166
  only used for assigned seating, 166
  personalization of, 243
plants, potted
  as guest favors, 88, 94
  to set off the area for exchanging vows,
    259
postage stamps, personalized, Zazzle as source
  for, 19, 53
procession, 153

ranunculus as a flower choice, 130
readings at ceremony, 186
reception, 168
  Beach Bliss themed ideas, 126–36
    buffets at beach themed weddings,
      133
  Boho style themed ideas, 269–79
  choosing a different dress for, 155
  creating a grand entrance to, 88–89, 167
  Farmhouse Rustic themed ideas, 82–98
  Free Spirit themed ideas, 202–14
  grand exit/send off, 52, 175, 214, 250
  providing a lounge area, 270
  providing transportation from ceremony
    to, 152, 261
  Romantically Vintage themed ideas, 40–52
  tented receptions, 20, 46, 63, 126–27, 128,
    145, 240, 241
  Traditional Wedding themed ideas, 240–50
  traditions for, 247
  Urban Chic themed ideas, 164–75
reception card, 219, 220
recessional, 228
reply cards/reply postcards, 12, 107

resorts as wedding locations, 110, 112
restaurants as wedding locations, 126, 143
ribbon cakes, 278
ribbons
  ribbon wand for flower girl, 113, 148
  use of as aisle decor, 257
  use of to create a focal point, 22
  use of to create a theme, 19, 25
  use of to display seating locations, 86
rice, alternatives to throwing See confetti;
  seeds for throwing
ring bearer, 120, 236
  attire for
    Bitsy Blossom as source for shoes,
      265, 280
    casual choices for a beach wedding,
      121
    as miniature groomsman, 78, 160,
      198, 236
    ways to reflect a specific era, 35
  gifts for, 27, 72
    "ring bearer badge," Knotty Notions as
      source for, 231, 251
    "ring-bearer cape," 152
    toys and books, 152, 231
  having more than one, 149
  role in a traditional wedding, 229
  unconventional choices to carry, 188–89,
    261
    carrying a memento instead of ring,
      148
    nautical themed, 113
    rustic themed, 71
  vintage themed materials to carry, 25
ring pillows
  sources for alternatives
    Lucky You Lucky Me, 113, 137
    LV Woodworks, 148, 175
  unconventional choices, 25, 71–72, 113,
    148, 188–89, 261
    use of a "ring bag" instead, 229
    use of a wooden box instead, 148, 261
ring warming ceremony, 187
rings, tattooed, 187
rooftop as wedding location, 139, 143, 146,
  164
roses as a flower choice, 239, 266
RSVPs to e-mail, 107
rugs, use of as aisle runners, 23
runners
  aisle runners, 23, 68, 224, 257
    alternatives to, 147
    monograms used on, 224
    ombre style petals, 147
    Sparkle Soiree as source for colored
      silk petals, 147, 175
    vintage materials to use, 23
  table runners, 91, 130, 169
    burlap for texture, 47
    choosing patterns to reflect wedding
      theme, 169
    moss as, 86
Rust-Oleum, 46, 261, 271, 280

sand ceremony, 146
sand dollar
  in bouquets or boutonniers, 123, 125
  as escort card and favor, 127
  faux sand dollar as cake decoration, 135
  as guest book alternative, 129
  sand dollar "dish" as ring pillow, 113
save-the-date cards, 16, 16–17, 56, 102
  examples of, 103, 104, 105, 142, 179,
    180, 181
  free-spirited themes reflected in, 178–80
  giving hint of a bohemian theme, 254
  mail early for out-of-town weddings, 12
  not always necessary, 220
  sources for
    Hoopla Love, 142, 175
    Mavora Art and Design, 104, 137
    Pistachio Press, 17, 53
    Starboard Press, 104, 137
    Wide Eyes Design, 104, 137
seashells, 125, 129
  as aisle runner or decor, 111, 113
  in bouquets or boutonniers, 123, 125
  as cake toppers, By the Seashore Decor as
    source for, 135, 137

chocolate seashell candies, Andie's
  Specialty Sweets as source for, 135, 137
flower girl carrying, 113
as motif for beach wedding, 114, 135, 136
as reception decorations, 127
ring bearer using to carry ring, 113
shell-shaped soaps as favors, Soap Cafe as
  source for, 136, 137
sources for
  The Bridal Flower, 123, 137
  Shell Outlet, 123, 137
as substitute for guest book, 129
used as an alternative in ring warming
  ceremony, 187
used in jewelry, 119
seating
  at the ceremony, 69, 223
    arrangement of chairs, 147
    on the beach, 111
    Chiavari as source for, 147, 175
    creating a free-spirit feeling in a
      backyard wedding, 185
    using a "ghost chair," 146–47
    using nontraditional or mismatched
      seating, 23
  at the reception, incorporating vintage
    charm, 46–47
  sweetheart table/head table, 46
seeds for throwing, 70, 153
sequins and glitter
  sequined wand for flower girl, 148–49
  use of as aisle runners, 147
  use of as table runners, 169
shells See seashells
shepherd's hook, use of as decoration, 23,
  68, 89
shoes, 16
  and "blue tradition," 228
  for the bride, 104, 155, 156, 194, 194,
    233, 263
    choice of to avoid snagging or
      tripping, 68, 75
    choosing sandals or barefeet at beach
      wedding, 111
    Western style boots as a choice for
      rustic wedding, 75
  for the groom, 31, 159, 197, 235
  shoe accessories, 30
  shoebox as place to put guests' shoes if
    wedding is on beach, 115
  sources for
    Beach Foot Jewelry, 118
    Bitsy Blossom for children's shoes,
      265, 280
    Converse, 197, 215
    Dr. Martens, 197, 215
    New Bride Co., 75, 99
    TOMS shoes, 194, 215
    Zappos, 194, 215
  for the wedding party, 77, 121, 122, 156,
    195, 235, 230, 265, 265, 265
signage, 65
  decorating the sweetheart table, 46,
    275, 275
  to direct to ceremony or reception, 40,
    64, 65, 115
    for areas within the reception, 167
  flower girl carrying sign rather than
    flowers, 71, 113
  using chalkboard/signage, 271
    to assign seating, 12, 85, 86, 127, 204
    The Seating Chart Boutique as source
      for, 127, 137
silverware and custom stamping, Wooden Hive
  as source for, 50, 53
soaps, 49
  as favors for guests, 49, 94, 136, 172,
    210, 277
    anchor-shaped soaps, 136
    shell-shaped soaps, 136
  as gifts for the wedding party, 72
  sources for
    Latika Soap, 136, 137
    Soap Cafe, 136, 137
    Vice & Velvet, 172, 175
sola flowers, 66, 80, 90
  sources for
    Etsy, 66, 99
    Roxy Heart Vintage, 66, 99

solar lanterns, 89–90
"something old, something new," 227
spa visit as gift, 230
sparkler send-off from a beach reception, 136
stamps
  personalizing postage stamps at Zazzle,
    19, 53
  sources of vintage stamps
    Champion Stamp Company, 19, 53
    eBay, 19, 53
    Kenmore Stamp Company, 19, 53
Star Wars as a wedding theme, 183, 188, 189,
  198, 208, 210, 214
starfish
  in boutonniers, 125
  faux starfish as cake decoration, 135
  as hair accessory, 118
  jewelry incorporating, 119
  as motif for beach wedding, 12, 104,
    114, 123
  raffia and starfish chair hanger
    137, 111
    Beach Weddings by Bree as source
      for, 111
stationery, 102–5, 107–8, 254–55 See also
  ceremony program; escort cards; invitations;
  place cards; reply cards/reply postcards;
  save-the-date cards; table numbers; thank-
  you cards
  creating bold, modern looks, 140–42
  creating traditional and "modern"
    traditional looks, 218–20
  examples of, 17, 18, 19, 56, 58, 59, 60,
    103, 105, 109, 140, 141, 142, 179, 180,
    181, 219, 255
  free-spirited themes reflected in, 178–80
  sources for
    Amanda Day Rose, 19, 53, 57, 58,
      59, 99
    Blue Magpie Invitations, 255, 280
    Crafty Pie Press, 180, 215
    Daydream Prints, 141, 175
    Ello There, 17, 53
    Hoopla Love, 142, 175, 255, 280
    Jen Simpson Design, 17, 19, 53, 60,
      99, 141, 175, 219, 251, 255, 280
    LetterBoxInk, 180, 215
    M3 and Co., 179, 215
    Mavora Art and Design, 104, 137
    Pistachio Press, 17, 53
    Ruff House Art, 179, 215
    Serendipity Beyond Design, 105, 137,
      141, 175
    Shine Wedding Invitations, 219, 251
    Sparkvites, 100, 215
    Starboard Press, 104, 137
    {via}various Designs, 107, 137
    Wide Eyes Design, 104, 137
    Wood & Grain, 57, 60, 99
  stationery suites, 12, 13, 17, 19, 56–58,
    108, 140–42, 210–19, 254–55
    escort cards/place cards/table
      numbers as part of, 270
    including a personal photo, 58, 99
steampunk as a wedding theme, 179, 189, 190,
  192, 193, 194–95, 199, 200, 212, 213
straws, bright colored for reception use, 17
  Cute Tape as source for, 128, 137
"submerged" centerpieces, 245
succulents as a flower choice
  for bouquets or boutonniers, 80, 162, 163
  for cake stand, 96
  for centerpieces or table decorations, 90,
    92, 169, 170
  as favors for guests, 172
suitcases, use of in design, 22, 276
  used as the card box, 44
sunflowers as a flower choice, 79, 239
sunglasses
  oversized as prop for photo booth, 51
  provide for a beach wedding, 116
  as quirky accessory for wedding party, 197
sweetheart table/head table, 172, 172, 247,
  275
  choosing chairs that are different from
    guests' chairs, 275
  signage decorating, 46, 275
  traditional wedding calling for a head
    table for wedding party, 247

table decor, 168, 169 See also centerpieces
  creating foundation through tablecloth
    choices, 272
  sources for vintage china
    Vintage Dish Rental, 272, 280
    Vintage Plate Rental, 272, 280
  traditional wedding requiring elegant and
    formal decor, 244
table numbers, 43
  alternatives to numbers, 12, 166, 204, 243
  and centerpieces, 206
    complimenting the centerpiece style,
      243
  making your own, 204
  matching to the escort cards, 270
  rustic themed ideas for creating, 87
  use of as part of centerpiece, 47, 170
tablecloth choices laying foundation for table
  decor, 272
tattoos, temporary as favors, 209
teacup roses, 163
teacups
  for centerpieces, 47
  as favors for guests, 277
teapots, use of as decorations, 19, 47
  for centerpieces, 47, 49
  flower girl carrying, 25
teas in muslin bags as favors for guests, 277
"tea-stained" aged effect, use of, 19
telegram as save-the-date card, 17
temporary tattoos as favors, 209
tented receptions, 20, 46, 63, 126–27, 128,
  145, 240, 241
test-tube vials to hold centerpiece flowers, 130
thank-you cards, 13
  leaving notes at guests' seats, 44, 270
  using photos from the reception, 46
theater stage as wedding location, 145, 183
thoughtful extras for guests, 115–16, 152–53
tickets to a sporting event as a gift for
  groomsmen, 151
toasts, 83, 231, 242, 247, 275
toys and books as gifts for flower girl and ring
  bearer, 27, 72, 152, 231
transportation, 191, 231
  choosing offbeat styles, 191, 261
  for guests, 152, 261
trees as a motif, 58 See also wood, use of as
  decoration
  as focal point for the exchange of vows, 66
  tree slice
    as an alternative guest book, 93
    as a cake stand, 98
    coasters as gifts, 72
    as part of centerpieces, 92, 130
    as ring "pillow," 71
  tree stumps for aisle decoration, 67
  "tree" thumbprint guest book, 93
tulips as a flower choice, 237
twigs
  twig cake topper, 98
  twig pencil, 93
twinkle lights, 241
typewriter, use of
  for creating guest book comments, 45
  to identify table assignments, 42
typography, use of to create the theme, 17, 19

unity ceremony, 146
U.S. Postal Service approving personalized
  stamps from Zazzle, 19, 53

vegetables, use of as decorations, 67, 79
veils, 233
  adding handmade touches to, 264
  alternatives to, 74, 118, 155, 193, 264
  need to fasten against wind at the beach,
    118
  tradition that mother puts the veil on the
    bride, 234
  types of for vintage look, 30
venues, 61–63, 256
  beach weddings, 110
  big cities as a choice, 143
  changing ceremony space into reception
    space, 164
  choosing spots around water, 126–27
  church as a traditional choice, 220

traditional choices for the reception, 240
  types of packages available, 222
vineyard as site for wedding, 20
vows, exchange of, 20
  creating a vow box, 70
  examples of, 221, 223
  focal point for exchange of vows, 20, 21,
    22, 65–66, 112, 225, 259
  use of unconventional vows or readings,
    186

warehouses as wedding locations, 143, 144
weather and outdoor weddings, 62, 63, 115,
  126, 145, 222, 241
wedding cake, 50, 96, 134, 135, 212, 213
  alternatives to, 98
    cupcakes, 97, 174, 213, 279
    dessert bar, 172, 174, 250, 258
  cutting the cake, 279
  groom's cake, 175, 213
  minimalist look for, 174
  number of tiers for a traditional cake, 250
  romantic, fantasy-style cakes, 278–79
wedding couple, photos of, 5, 34, 52, 54, 70,
  102, 117, 136, 138, 144, 153, 184, 187, 202,
  218, 221, 223, 252, 254
wedding party, 31, 61, 119, 178, 197, 216,
  226, 264 See also specific attendants, i.e.,
  bridesmaids, ring bearer, etc.,
    gifts for, 26–27, 150–52, 190, 230–31
    "wedding-party plans," 248–49
wedding toasts, 83, 231, 242, 247, 275
wedding traditions, 227–28
  getting-ready tradition, 234
  nontraditional traditions, 187
  pearls as traditional bride choice, 233
  relating to choice of bridal gown, 232
  relating to the wedding cake, 250
  relating to transportation, 231
  traditional dances, 247–48
Western style wedding, 75, 76, 77, 98
wheat
  for bouquets or boutonniers, 79, 123, 125
  as a motif for a farm or country wedding,
    59
whimsical wedding decorations, 17, 67, 104,
  149, 186, 196, 206, 214, 272, 277
windows, weathered, use of as decorations, 22
  showing table assignments on window
    panes, 42, 86
wines
  Scissor Mill as source for glasses, 146, 175
  wine as gift for bridesmaids, 26, 150
  wine ceremony, 146
  wine motif for a traditional wedding, 242
  wine-bottle buoy charms for favors, 136
  wineglass charms as escort cards, 203
winter weddings, flower choices for, 162
wood, use of as decoration See also trees as
  a motif
  as a cake stand, 96
  log used as candle holder, 92
  as napkin holders, 92
  planter box or crate as centerpieces, 92
  for signs, 46, 65, 71, 89
  table runners, 91
  used in an arch, 65
  using planks, 87
  weathering of, Rust-Oleum as a paint
    treatment, 261, 280
  wooden bench as an alternative guest
    book, 93
  wooden boxes, 70, 148, 172
  wooden heart charm, 75
  wooden monograms, 93
  wooden numbers, 43, 87
  wooden trays, 86, 90
    as table runners, 91–92
  wooden vases, Heirloom Woodwork as
    source for, 130, 137
woodland setting as a wedding location, 55,
  59, 60, 61, 62, 63, 65, 66, 73, 79, 82, 86
woven grass, 257

yarn balls as decorations, 90, 199
  in bouquets, 199, 200
  in boutonniers, 199, 199

zoo as a wedding location, 182–83, 213

# Acknowledgments

Thank you to Robin Haywood and Charlotte Cromwell of Sellers Publishing, Inc., who offered their expertise and insight every step of the way. It is an honor to work with such an amazing team. Thank you to Renee Rooks Cooley for proofreading and Laura Shelley for indexing this book. Thank you to Sellers Publishing, Inc., for publishing *The Inspired Wedding*. A big high five to Marilyn Allen, my agent, who helped me with this opportunity. I am so grateful. Thank you to the photographers who so kindly contributed their images to this book, especially Michelle Gardella, Eric Boneske, Carolyn Scott, Geoff Brown, Justin Battenfield, and Shillawna Ruffner. You truly bring these pages to life! Thank you to the artisans whose handmade work continues to inspire me on a daily basis. Thank you to my husband, Andrew, who offers endless support, enthusiasm, and laughs; and to Andrew Francis, my son, who has brought so much joy. I love you both with all my heart. Thank you to Mom and Dad for always cheering me on — I'm blessed to have the best parents in the world. Much love to you both! Thank you to my sister, Elise, who always manages to work Emmaline Bride into conversation. Love you, sis! I would also like to thank the rest of my family and my friends, who are always a source of encouragement — I am grateful to be surrounded by such wonderful people. And finally, a big thank-you goes out to the readers of Emmaline Bride — without all of you, none of this would be possible.

-Emma Arendoski
www.emmaarendoski.com